OCT. 9 1968

6809559

822.09 WEBSTER

3

RABKIN

TWENTIETH CENTURY INTERPRETA-
TIONS OF THE DUCHESS OF MALFI

WAYNE PUBLIC LIBRARY

MAIN LIBRARY

475 Valley Road
Wayne, N. J. 07470

Books may be returned at any
branch of the library.

D1609315

TWENTIETH CENTURY
INTERPRETATIONS

MAYNARD MACK, *Series Editor*
Yale University

NOW AVAILABLE
Collections of Critical Essays
ON

TWENTIETH CENTURY INTERPRETATIONS
OF

THE DUCHESS
OF MALFI

6809559

TWENTIETH CENTURY INTERPRETATIONS
OF

THE DUCHESS
OF MALFI

A Collection of Critical Essays

Edited by
NORMAN RABKIN

Prentice-Hall, Inc.   A SPECTRUM BOOK   *Englewood Cliffs, N. J.*

Copyright © 1968 by Prentice-Hall, Inc., Englewood Cliffs, New Jersey. A
SPECTRUM BOOK. All rights reserved. No part of the book may be reproduced
in any form or by any means without permission in writing from the publisher.
Library of Congress Catalog Card Number 68-17830. Printed in the United States
of America.

Current Printing (last number):
10 9 8 7 6 5 4 3 2 1

Contents

Introduction

by Norman Rabkin

I.

John Webster may have been born in 1580. The only reason we have to think so is that twenty-two would be a likely age for the playwright first listed in the records of the theatrical entrepreneur Henslowe as receiving payment in 1602. He may have died before November, 1634, though our only reason for thinking so is a rather shaky interpretation of the tenses Thomas Heywood uses in describing some of his contemporaries in a poem licensed in that month; or he may have been the John Webster whose death is recorded in a London burial register on March 3, 1637/8. "How came Antonio by his death?" asks Malateste at the end of *The Duchess of Malfi*; the only answer he gets from the man who knows best is "In a mist: I know not how." Nor do we know much more about the years of the poet's flourishing. We are sure of his authorship of the two great tragedies, of a tragicomedy, *The Devil's Law Case,* which no one can date with assurance, of commendatory verses, a pageant, and an induction. We have record of his collaboration with other dramatists on a number of plays, but many of those plays are lost, and few scholars agree about the extent of Webster's participation in the rest. Such ignorance is only an extreme version of the state of our knowledge about other playwrights of the period.

The little we do know, however, makes it possible to construct a surprisingly clear picture, a paradoxical element of which is the playwright's apparent anonymity. That picture is of a kind of man new to English letters, one who had made his first appearance in the generation of Marlowe, Kyd, Lyly, and Shakespeare in the two decades preceding Webster's arrival: the professional playwright. Like the "University Wits" of the first generation and his contemporary Ben Jonson, Webster seems to have come from middle-class origins (by his own word he was a merchant-tailor). Like most dramatists of the period he was educated well but not at the universities. He appears to have written, like all of his colleagues, to pay the grocer, and to have been available for odd jobs: as Jonson refurbished Kyd's *Spanish Tragedy* for a new

audience, so Webster added some touches to Marston's *Malcontent,*
played originally by one of the children's companies, to adapt it for
the more plebeian audience of the King's Men. Like Jonson, Middleton, Dekker, and Heywood, most of whom collaborated with him on
various occasions, Webster wrote with equal facility in the radically
different modes of the private children's theater and the public men's
companies, bridging the worlds of Marston and Shakespeare. The record suggests close friendship with at least one co-worker, the prodigious Heywood, continuous involvement in the theater for at least
two decades, and an ability to create in all the modes decreed by the
rapidly changing fashions of early seventeenth-century drama: chron-
icle, Roman tragedy, satirical London comedy, Fletcherian tragicomedy, and tragedy.

Webster's versatility is what makes his facelessness significant rather
than simply frustrating. Some of the principal dramatists of the period
—Marlowe, Shakespeare, Chapman, Marston, Jonson—are identifiable
in the clearly marked progress of a powerful and single sensibility.
Others—most notably Beaumont and Fletcher—establish their identi-
ties through their fashion-setting dedication (à la Alfred Hitchcock)
to a brilliant and habitual way of playing on a rather narrow set of
conventions. But Webster belongs to a third group that comprises the
majority of the playwrights of the period. Like Heywood and Middleton, Dekker and Massinger, Webster manifests his talent in a high
level of competence at whatever the mode of the day or the manage-
ment of a theater leads him to try, in certain consistent formal and
stylistic habits which seem more like fingerprints than like attempts
to impose his will on the material [1] and above all in the ability to
emerge for brief and unforgettable moments, when the conventions in
which he is writing coincide with personal predilection, as an extraordinarily personal writer whose triumphs send us on a fruitless
search to find the man behind the work.

One is hard put to relate *The White Devil* and *The Duchess of Malfi*
to the landscape from which they emerge, but no more so than is the
case when one sees Middleton's magnificent tragedy *The Changeling*
against its background of cynical city comedies, lumbering Fletcherian
tragicomedies, and Italianate villain-drama, or Heywood's rare triumphs in tragedy and comedy against the incredibly numerous and
diverse plays of which they are the best. The mystery is only half a
mystery of the artist's personality; the other half is the phenomenon of
a thriving art which, involving the best talents of an army of artists in
work that is generally run-of-the-mill, makes possible to men who are
no Shakespeares dazzling and unaccountable moments in the sun.

---

[1] See, for example, Inga-Stina Ekeblad, "Webster's Constructional Rhythm,"
XXIV (1957), 165-76.

Without Webster, needless to say, there would have been no *Duchess of Malfi*; yet thirty years earlier a poet whose chief characteristic most of the time is a sensitivity to the possibilities latent in the going conventions could not have written a play remotely like it, and thirty years later playwrights of equal competence and similar habits of composition—Ford, Shirley—could scarcely make the conventions serve them.

II.

As one might expect, then, one learns more about *The Duchess of Malfi* by seeing it in its place in contemporary theater than one might if one knew a good deal more about its author's life. Webster's two tragedies virtually end the only sustained period in which the London theater produced tragedies. By the time he turned to them, in the years between 1609 and 1613, the tragedies of Marlowe, Peele, Kyd, Chettle, Chapman, Jonson, Marston, Heywood, and Shakespeare were already behind him. Middleton was to write his astonishing *Changeling* in 1622 and *Women Beware Women* perhaps in the same year, and Ford's two fine tragedies were to appear later in that decade, but, with the exception of a few such resurgences, the form as the Elizabethans had created it seems to have been approaching collapse as Webster began his work. After Webster most plays styled tragedy and accepted as such by their audiences are only technically distinguishable from Fletcherian tragicomedy, or, like Shirley's *Cardinal* (1641), fecklessly imitate conventions emptied of any meaning.

Speculation on why the Jacobeans lost interest in tragedy demands more space than is here available, but several facts are clear. The older tragedy—even the apparently irreverent tragedy of Marlowe—had assumed enough about the permanence of order, social and cosmic, to make possible at least a dialectical balancing of order against disorder. If Elizabethan revenge tragedy questioned the heavens' ability to right earthly wrongs, it presented at any rate a conviction that those heavens stood ultimately in some genuine relation to what happened beneath them. But in the late Shakespeare such a notion is increasingly a question rather than an assumption. As early a tragedy as *Hamlet* makes us wonder whether the order purchased at the end is worth the price paid for it, and the last tragedies scarcely pretend to console their audience for the loss of what they teach that audience to admire. The increasingly dominant modes of Jacobean drama offer their audience satirical rejection of the world or sentimental retreat from it. The death of tragedy is the death of the sense that one dare confront the most serious issues, and, if not resolve them, at least live comfortably in their presence. Paradoxically, the power of dramatists to imitate in tragedy the lonely struggles of heroic individuals vanishes with the sense of commonwealth, of shared values and community that informed the earlier drama. In Shakespeare's work the pairing of these rival and essential elements of tragedy reaches its most poignant embodiment in *Othello, Lear,* and *Macbeth*; in *Antony and Cleopatra* and *Coriolanus* both hero and society are so defective as to change the nature of tragedy, and Shakespeare turns to romance. Doubtless the causes of the decline of tragedy are social, and our understanding of the history of the drama has been coming in recent years to include a haunting awareness of a singular fact: by the time of King James' accession in 1603, a civil war which was really a revolution—social, intellectual, political, and spiritual—was less than four decades away and already in the making.

One phenomenon in which we recognize the new loss of faith in the old order is the growing conviction of such tragic dramatists as remained in prerevolutionary England that the heroic virtue of the individual celebrated in Elizabethan tragedy is no longer relevant. Increasingly tragedy presents helpless men whose heroism is ironically qualified by the contexts in which they live. Othello and Lear are the victims of gigantic conspiracies as well as of themselves; but Macbeth and Antony and Coriolanus, more strikingly, are ruined in large part by women. And Webster inaugurates a new fashion (perhaps abetted by Fletcher): he signifies the final helplessness of his tragic protagonists by making them women. The pattern will continue in the best tragedies of the period until the theaters close at the outbreak of the war. The emergence of "she-tragedy" is as clear a sign of the passing of a system of values as the disappearance of Renaissance tragedy.

III.

Like *The White Devil, The Duchess of Malfi* is quirky. Much of what troubles critics who dislike it stems from their failure to recognize how much of the play is conventional or from their rejection of the conventions they recognize. On the other hand, Webster seems to go out of his way to exaggerate those conventions. Think of the characteristic trick, for example, of setting the dramatis personae in the roles of choric commentators, describing each other in formal "characters" like character-books come to life; or of the luridness, excessive even for the theater in which *Titus Andronicus* had made its success, of such devices as the set of wax figures representing the Duchess' murdered family, the severed hand, the poisoned book, the apricot test for pregnancy, the masque of madmen; or the emphasis Webster gives to the passage of enough time between Acts Two and Three for the

Duchess to have borne two children—a time that Delio remarks seems scarcely half an hour; or the echo scene; or Ferdinand's lycanthropy. Note also Webster's magpie style, his constant and constantly ostentatious borrowing from other writers; and the broken-backed structure of the play, throwing away its heroine a full act before the end. The play has, in fact, an operatic quality beyond anything else in its period; it looks forward to nothing so much as to the crazy Verdi plots loaded with intrigue and gypsies, night and death, blatant coincidence and scenes constructed primarily for their sensational effects. More like opera than like other Renaissance drama, *The Duchess of Malfi* is built to move toward great lyric moments: Ferdinand's "Cover her face: mine eyes dazzle: she died young"; Bosola's bellman song.

And as in Verdian opera, the vital paradox of the play is the discrepancy between the improbable plot and conventions on the one hand and the utter integrity of the moral vision and the imaginative world on the other. The plot perches continually on the edge of ludicrousness; yet the characters, once again like Verdi's, operate according to their creator's profound understanding of humanity and his refusal to sentimentalize and idealize. As the disagreement among critics will testify, Webster's characters are rich, complex, and mysterious. Bosola, successor to Flamineo of *The White Devil,* is a deeper character than his model. A weak man but, at least at first, one who does not deceive himself, he differs immediately from the stock Machiavellian villain because he is one against his conscience. Established at the outset as a choric commentator whose perceptiveness demands our assent, he succumbs with disturbing alacrity to the money and position that Ferdinand offers him; but he has the good sense to hate himself for his compromise, and as a result becomes a version of another stock character, the malcontent, whose most positive quality is hatred of the world. Webster deepens the characterization by planting the roots of malcontent in a self-hatred so paralyzing that Bosola can repent, despite his frequent qualms, only after he has murdered the Duchess, and by mirroring Bosola's spiritual helplessness in the accident proneness of a born loser who cannot help but kill Antonio despite (or because of) his good intentions.

Similar integrity governs the characterization of the Duchess' villainous brothers. Ferdinand terrifies us most in his total unawareness of the real springs of his action. Though critics continue to debate the incestuousness of his passion, and though attempts to translate the perceptions of seventeenth-century writers into the language of twentieth-century psychology all too often distort literary facts, the inescapable peculiarity of Ferdinand's passion is the disproportion between its intensity and the financial reasons which he seems to believe set him against his sister's remarriage. The violence of his language in the great scene in Act One in which he and the Cardinal forbid the Duchess to remarry is startling enough; but the tone of his speech later when, hearing that his sister has given birth, he imagines her vividly in the act of carnal sin (ii. v. 42ff.), forces us to hear more than he intends. The closest equivalent in the drama of the period is Hamlet's response to his mother's remarriage. The violence of Ferdinand's responses suggests the incestuous motivation that figures more explicitly in Beaumont and Fletcher's *A King and No King* and Ford's *'Tis Pity She's a Whore*. His later retreat into the pathological condition of lycanthropy is a fitting dramatic image for what Webster has conveyed through language.

Even more terrifying is the figure of the Cardinal. Unlike Ferdinand he seems dispassionate, cold, rational; his character would seem to be summed up in his treatment of Julia: he lies to her, ruins her, and kills her. Again unlike his brother he is psychologically acute himself. He is sensitive to the excessiveness of Ferdinand's passion, and he is able to formulate, as part of his callous strategy against the pathetic Julia, a notion of psychological projection that would do credit to any psychoanalyst (ii. iv. 10-12). What is frightening about the Cardinal is what disturbs us in so many of Shakespeare's villains: his superficial rationality, which he never surrenders, masks a compulsive nihilism every bit as irrational and destructive as Ferdinand's. As modern politics teaches us every day, no madness is so terrible as that which views itself as reasonable and is so accepted by the world.

The world of *The Duchess of Malfi* is a world of authority figures driven by compulsions they scarcely sense themselves, in which a Bosola's awareness of the moral implications of his own actions has no binding power on that action and the imagery underlines the plot's insistence that abnormality is the norm. It is a world of utter depravity wearing the mask of ordered society, of universal hypocrisy on a tragic level such as Ben Jonson had portrayed on the comic. And into this world Webster brings his Duchess, a gallant woman brave enough to live as she thinks right.

As the essays that follow will show, there is no common agreement as to how Webster's audience felt about second marriages when they contemplated the matter abstractly, or about duchesses marrying beneath their station. But surely in the play there is no question.[2] An emblem that concentrates much of what Webster wants us to feel occurs when the Duchess, left alone to brush her hair after a touchingly relaxed and innocent conversation with her husband and her servant, notices that she is growing gray and speculates on the peaceful years she sees lying ahead of her, only to be interrupted by the savage Ferdi-

---

[2] One might note that no one has ever criticized Dame Christian Custance in *Roister Doister* for *her* second marriage.

nand, who gives her a dagger to kill herself. We admire the courage with which she leaves her life, in contrast to her craven servant who wants to cling to life at any cost and in contrast again to the quiet desperation in which her unheroic husband meets his end; the Duchess at the end of the play, or at least of her part in it, is an unforgettable figure. But to judge from the testimony of the critics the image that lingers longest is that of the poignant hairbrushing scene, with all its implications of the explosion of the world of innocence.

The deepest irony of *The White Devil* is the fact that Webster finds heroic qualities appropriate to a character who is both a woman and a villain. In that irony there is a Marlovian bumptiousness, associating heroic virtue with moral wickedness and letting the audience sort out the resultant chaos at its own risk. But the irony of *The Duchess of Malfi* is both deeper and clearer. It consists in the creation of one of the purest, strongest, and most admirable of tragic heroes, whose life is consistently presented in terms of the image of a voyage (not unlike Othello's "pilgrimage"), whose heroic mission constitutes no more than the desire to live the life of a good bourgeoise. Now such a paradox clearly signals the end of tragic value. In its ironic celebration of the joys of an unavailable world of everyday life *The Duchess of Malfi* is a virtual antitragedy. Just as clearly it signals the end of a civilization, for the life that it presents as desirable it presents as unattainable, crushed by all the forces of destiny and character and a society whose norms are without informing energy. As witty on the grand scale as Donne's lyrics on the small, Webster's play turns upside down the values of conventional tragedy and normal social life in order to tell us that both are finished. Hence our constant sense of appropriateness as we respond to the imagery of night and birds, of screeching animals and rampant disease. This is the world that we have come to expect in prerevolutionary writers who know that one age is over and cannot envision a way out of it; it is the world of Dostoevsky and Nietzsche.

IV.

For its first audiences, sophisticated enough to recognize how Webster was playing on conventions that as long ago as *Titus Andronicus* had been deployed with all the self-consciousness of grand guignol, yet deeply sympathetic with such doubts as Webster voiced for them, *The Duchess of Malfi* must have been a complex experience, no doubt strangely satisfying yet powerfully uncomfortable. For us it is similarly uncomfortable, but more profitably so than it was to such a rationalist reader as the Ibsenite Archer. In our encounters with recent drama—the work of Harold Pinter, for example—we have discovered analogues to a play which toys with our expectations that a conventional form will lead us to a conventional conclusion. Recognition of the kinship between *The Duchess of Malfi* and some of the absurdist drama of the past few years may help readers avoid traps into which some critics have repeatedly fallen, and may provide a concept of the play which makes academic attempts to moralize and tame the play into Christian orthodoxy appear as superfluous as it does earlier tendencies to reject Webster's conventions as unselfconsciously "barbarous."

The essays that follow represent a cross-section of the attitudes toward *The Duchess of Malfi* that the twentieth century has produced, and of the ways in which scholarship has attempted to damn it or praise it or distort it or—best of all—to make it available to us. It will be clear from what has already been said that the editor himself has strong predilections. But it is a sign of Webster's strength that no essay in the collection, no matter how much the editor may disagree with it or how successfully another essay in the volume may quarrel with it, is without its strong basis in some aspect of the play itself.

PART ONE

Interpretations

Webster and *The Duchess of Malfi*

by Rupert Brooke

After the death of the Duchess, there is a slight lull before the rest of the tragedy rises again to its climax. It contains a queer scene of *macabre* comedy where Ferdinand beats his fantastic doctor, and a curious, rather Gothic, extraneous scene of quietness, where Antonio talks to the echo. The end is a maze of death and madness. Webster's supreme gift is the blinding revelation of some intense state of mind at a crisis, by some God-given phrase. All the last half of *The Duchess of Malfi* is full of them. The mad Ferdinand, stealing across the stage in the dark, whispering to himself, with the devastating impersonality of the madman, "Strangling is a very quiet death," is a figure one may not forget. And so in the next scene, the too sane Cardinal:—

> How tedious is a guilty conscience!
> When I look into the fish-ponds in my garden
> Methinks I see a thing armed with a rake
> That seems to strike at me.

It is one of those pieces of imagination one cannot explain, only admire.

But it is, of course, in or near the moment of death that Webster is most triumphant. He adopts the romantic convention, that men are, in the second of death, most essentially and significantly themselves. In the earlier play [*The White Devil*] the whole angry, sickening fear of death that a man feels who has feared nothing else, lies in those terrific words of Brachiano's when it comes home to him that he is fatally poisoned:—

> On pain of death, let no man name death to me:
> It is a word infinitely terrible.

"*Webster and* The Duchess of Malfi" *by Rupert Brooke. From* John Webster and the Elizabethan Drama (*London and New York: John Lane Ltd., 1916*).

Webster knows all the ways of approaching death. Flamineo, with the strange carelessness of the dying man, grows suddenly noble. "What dost think on?" his murderer asks him.

> *Flamineo.* Nothing; of nothing; leave thy idle questions.
>   I am i' the way to study a long silence:
>   To prate were idle. I remember nothing.
>   There's nothing of so infinite vexation
>   As man's own thoughts.

And Webster, more than any man in the world, has caught the soul just in the second of its decomposition in death, when knowledge seems transcended, and the darkness closes in, and boundaries fall away.

> "My soul," cries Vittoria, "like to a ship in a black storm,
>   Is driven, I know not whither."

And Flamineo—

> While we look up to Heaven we confound
> Knowledge with knowledge, O, I am in a mist.

So in this play Ferdinand "seems to come to himself," as Bosola says, "now he's so near the bottom." He is still half-mad; but something of the old overweening claim on the universe fires up in the demented brain:

> Give me some wet hay: I am broken-minded.
> I do account this world but a dog-kennel:
> I will vault credit and affect high pleasures
> Beyond death.

*   *   *

The one influence upon Webster that is always noticeable is that of satire. His nature tended to the outlook of satire; and his plays give evidence that he read Elizabethan, and in some form Latin satire with avidity. *Hamlet,* the *Malcontent,* and all the heroes of that type of play, "railed" continually. But with Webster every character and nearly every speech has something of the satirical outlook. They describe each other satirically. They are for ever girding at the conventional objects of satire, certain social follies and crimes. There are several little irrelevant scenes of satire, like the malevolent discussion of Count Malatesti (*D.M.*, III. 3). It is incessant. The topics are the ordinary ones, the painting of women, the ingratitude of princes, the swaggering of blusterers, the cowardice of pseudo-soldiers. It gives part of the peculiar atmosphere of these plays.

This rests on a side of Webster's nature, which, in combination with

his extraordinary literary gifts, produces another queer characteristic
of his—his fondness for, and skill in comment. He is rather more like
a literary man trying to write for the theater than any of his contemporaries. Theatrically, though he is competent and sometimes powerful, he exhibits no vastly unusual ability. It is his comments that bite
deep. Such gems as Flamineo's description of Camillo:

> When he wears white satin one would take him by his black muzzle to
> be no other creature than a maggot;

or of the Spanish ambassador:

> He carries his face in's ruff, as I have seen a serving man carry glasses
> in a cipress hat-band, monstrous steady, for fear of breaking: he looks
> like the claw of a black-bird, first salted, and then broiled in a candle;

or Lodovico's of the black woman Zanche in love:

> Mark her, I prithee; she simpers like the suds
> A collier hath been washed in;

have frequently been quoted. They have a purely literary merit. In
other places he achieves a dramatic effect, which would be a little less
in a theater than in the book, by comment. When Bosola brings the
terrible discovery of the secret to Ferdinand and the Cardinal, he com-
municates it to them, unheard by us, upstage. We only know, in reading, how they take it, by the comments of Pescara, Silvio, and Delio,
who are watching, down-stage—

> *Pesc.*   Mark Prince Ferdinand:
> A very salamander lives in's eye,
> To mock the eager violence of fire.
> *Sil.* That cardinal hath made more bad faces with his oppression than
> ever Michael Angelo made good ones: he lifts up's nose like a foul
> porpoise before a storm.
> *Pes.* The Lord Ferdinand laughs.
> *Del.* Like a deadly cannon
> That lightens ere it smokes . . .

it goes straight to the nerves. "The Lord Ferdinand laughs." It is unforgettable.

Webster had always, in his supreme moments, that trick of playing
directly on the nerves. It is the secret of Bosola's tortures of the Duchess,
and of much of Flamineo. Though the popular conception of him is
rather one of immense gloom and perpetual preoccupation with death,
his power lies almost more in the intense, sometimes horrible, vigor
of some of his scenes, and his uncanny probing to the depths of the
heart. In his characters you see the instincts at work jerking and actuat-

ing them, and emotions pouring out irregularly, unconsciously, in floods or spurts and jets, driven outward from within, as you sometimes do in real people.

The method of progression which Webster used in his writing, from speech to speech or idea to idea, is curiously individual. The ideas do not develop into each other as in Shakespeare, nor are they tied together in neatly planned curves as in Beaumont and Fletcher. He seems to have, and we know he did, put them into the stream of thought from outside: plumping them down side by side. Yet the very cumbrousness of this adds, in a way, to the passion and force of his scenes, as a swift stream seems swifter and wilder when its course is broken by rocks and boulders. The craft of Shakespeare's genius moves with a speedy beauty like a yacht running close into the wind; Webster's is a barge quanted slowly but incessantly along some canal, cumbrous but rather impressive.

This quality of the progression of Webster's thought, and, in part, of his language, contrasts curiously with his meter. The Elizabethan use of blank verse was always liable to be rather fine; but there was only a short period, and it was only in a few writers, that it got really free—until its final dissolution in the thirties. Webster was one of these writers, probably the freest. Only Shakespeare can approach him in the liberties he took with blank verse; but Shakespeare's liberties conformed to higher laws. Webster probably had a worse ear for meter, at least in blank verse, than any of his contemporaries. His verse is perpetually of a vague, troubled kind. Each line tends to have about ten syllables and about five feet. It looks in the distance like a blank verse line. Sometimes this line is extraordinarily successful; though it is never quite scannable. Brachiano's

> It is a word infinitely terrible,

is tremendously moving. But sometimes Webster's metrical extravagance does not justify itself, and rather harasses. The trick of beginning a line with two unaccented syllables, if repeated too often in the same passage, does more to break the back of the meter than almost any other possible peculiarity.

On the whole it is probable that Webster did all this on purpose, seeing that a larger license of meter suits blank verse in drama than is permissible in literature. When he turned poet, in *A Monumental Column,* he is equally unmetrical; but that can probably be attributed to the very strong influence of Donne. Certainly the lyrics in his plays would seem to show that as a lyric poet he could have been among the greatest, a master of every subtlety, at least of that lyric meter which he did use. It is the one which the Elizabethans, almost, invented, and upon which they performed an inconceivable variety of music. Milton, who learned so much from them in this respect, made this meter the chief part of his heritage. But even he could not include all that various music. It is the meter of *L'Allegro, Il Penseroso,* and the end of *Comus.* No man ever got a stranger and more perfect melody from it than Webster in his dirges.

Webster's handling of a play, and his style of writing, have something rather slow and old-fashioned about them. He was not like Shakespeare or Beaumont and Fletcher, up-to-date and "slick." He worried his plays out with a grunting pertinacity. There are several uncouth characteristics of his that have an effect which halts between archaism and a kind of childish awkwardness, like "primitive" art of various nations and periods. Sometimes he achieves the same result it can have, of a simplicity and directness refreshingly different from later artifice and accomplishment. Sometimes he only seems, to the most kindly critic, to fail hopelessly for lack of skill. One of these characteristics is the use of couplets, usually to end the scene, and commonly of a generalizing nature. This is, of course, old-fashioned. The frequency of such couplets is an often-noticed feature of the early Elizabethan drama: and the plays of such a writer as Shakespeare are dated by the help of the percentage of rhyming to unrhyming lines. Even as late as Webster, other authors sometimes ended the play, or a scene, with a couplet. But they did it with grace; using it almost as a musical device, to bring the continued melody of their verse to a close. And in the earlier plays, where one or more rhyming couplets end most scenes and many speeches, and even, especially in the more lyrical parts, come into the middle of passages, the rest of the versification is of a simple, rhythmical end-stopped kind; and so the couplets seem scarcely different from the rest, a deeper shade of the same color. Webster's couplets are electric green or crimson, a violent contrast with the rough, jerky, sketchy blank verse he generally uses. . . .

The Duchess of Malfi

by William Archer

The long-delayed reaction against the cult of the lesser Elizabethans, initiated by Charles Lamb and caricatured by Swinburne, is being powerfully promoted by the activities of the Phoenix Society, which has recently been founded for the production of Elizabethan and Restoration plays. John Webster's *Duchess of Malfi*, revived last November at Hammersmith, had a very "bad Press." The privilege of listening to its occasional beauties of diction was felt to be dearly bought at the price of enduring three hours of coarse and sanguinary melodrama. But dramatic criticism in these days is so restricted in space that no one, so far as I have seen, has studied the structure of this famous "masterpiece," and shown that, even apart from its embroidery of horrors, the play is a fundamentally bad one. It is true that technical standards are not absolute, but vary in relation to the material conditions of the stage for which a play is designed. But even under Elizabethan conditions, there was nothing, except his singular inexpertness, to prevent Webster from telling his story well. Massinger, or even Middleton, would have made a very different thing of it.

There can be no doubt that the orthodox criticism of the past century placed *The Duchess of Malfi* only a little lower than Shakespeare's greatest tragedies. Lamb's eulogy I shall cite in its due place. For the present let us listen to Swinburne (*Age of Shakespeare*, pp. 15, 32):

> The crowning gift of imagination, the power to make us realize that thus and not otherwise it was, that thus and not otherwise it must have been, was given—except by exceptional fits and starts—to none of the poets of their time but only to Shakespeare and Webster . . . Except in Aeschylus, in Dante and in Shakespeare, I, at least, know not where to seek for passages which in sheer force of tragic and noble horror . . . may be set against the subtlest, the deepest, the sublimest passages of Webster.

"The Duchess of Malfi" by *William Archer. From* Nineteenth Century, *LXXXVII* (*1920*), *126-32. Copyright 1920 by* Nineteenth Century. *Reprinted by permission of* Twentieth Century.

Swinburne, it will be noted, ignores structure and development, and
centers his attention on "passages." Passage-worship is the vice of this
whole school of criticism.

Let us now recall to memory the main features of *The Duchess of
Malfi*. Lest I be suspected of misrepresenting the plot, I quote the sum-
mary of it given by a twentieth-century admirer, the lamented Rupert
Brooke (*John Webster and the Elizabethan Drama*, p. 97):

> The Duchess of Malfi is a young widow forbidden by her brothers
> Ferdinand and the Cardinal to marry again. They put a creature of
> theirs, Bosola, into her service as a spy. The Duchess loves and secretly
> marries her steward, Antonio, and has three children. Bosola ultimately
> discovers and reports this. Antonio and the Duchess have to fly. The
> Duchess is captured, imprisoned and mentally tortured, and put to death.
> Ferdinand goes mad. In the last act he, the Cardinal, Antonio and Bosola
> are all killed with various confusions and in various horror.

To this concisely accurate argument of the play I will only subjoin
that the butcher's bill is by no means complete. Brooke tells only of
five corpses: to these we must add the Cardinal's mistress Julia, two of
the Duchess's children, her maid Cariola, and a servant—ten in all.
The murders in *Hamlet* run to only half that number.

The First Act ushers us slowly into the theme, with a series of char-
acter-sketches of the Duchess and her two brothers, delivered by Antonio to his confidant, Delio. Then the "Arragonian brethren," as they
are called, coarsely and brutally warn their sister against marrying
again. It need scarcely be said that they are taking the best possible
means to make her defy their tyranny; but Webster might reply that
if all men were experts in feminine psychology, drama would disappear
both from life and from the stage. A more serious objection to their
conduct is that it has no assignable motive. There is not the smallest
reason why they should object to their sister's making an open and
honorable marriage. Towards the end of the play, this thought seems
to strike Ferdinand, and he tells us that

> He had a hope,
> Had she continued widow, to have gained
> An infinite mass of treasure.

But it is hard to guess how this can be, seeing that the Duchess has a
surviving son by her first marriage. This son, the reigning Duke of
Malfi, is only once alluded to: the Duchess herself seems quite to have
forgotten his existence: but it is at one point quite explicitly mentioned, and deprives the conduct of the Duke and Cardinal of the last
vestige of reason.

Be this as it may, the brethren instal Bosola, a disreputable soldier of fortune, as their spy or "intelligencer," and take themselves off. No sooner are their backs turned than the Duchess sends for Antonio, and, in a scene of some charm, proposes to him a secret union.

In the Second Act, we start a cumbersome underplot, concerned with the Cardinal's mistress, Julia, which serves no purpose except to provide us with a scene of lust and murder in the last Act. We presently find that the Duchess is about to give birth to a child, and that the lynx-eyed Bosola, though he suspects her condition, has no idea who is the father. We see him ferreting around the Duchess's apartments at the time of her lying-in; and his suspicions are confirmed when he picks up a calculation of the child's nativity which Antonio has casually dropped. What should we say of a modern dramatist who should bring about the revelation of a deadly secret through the inconceivable folly of a leading character, who first composes a compromising document, and then drops it in the actual presence of a man whom he knows to be a spy!

Bosola now takes Antonio to be accessory to the Duchess's amour (he expresses the idea more briefly); but he is apparently incapable of putting two and two together, and so does not suspect him of being the father of the child. He of course informs the Duke and the Cardinal of his discovery, and Ferdinand goes into an epilepsy of fury at the idea of "the royal blood of Arragon and Castile" being "thus attainted." He proposes to "lay her general territory waste," to "hew her to pieces," to "make a sponge of her bleeding heart," and to boil down her child into a broth and administer it to the unknown father. He is an agreeable gentleman, is Ferdinand, Duke of Calabria.

And now comes a curious and characteristic point. In spite of the foaming fury of the Arragonians, they do nothing at all to avenge their precious "honor," or to save it from further stains. They stand idly by for at least a couple of years, while the Duchess, at her leisure, bears two more children to Antonio! If there exists a common-sense principle so clear and compulsive that it may fairly be called a law, it is surely that a violent passion, once aroused, must "ne'er feel retiring ebb, but keep due on" till it has vented itself in destructive action. What should we say if a modern dramatist presented to us such a broken-backed play? It may be urged that Webster was only following his narrative source in giving the Duchess and Antonio three children. But he was under no obligation to follow it. His business was to compress the very prolix narrative, as it appears in Paynter's *Palace of Pleasure,* into a good play. And in Paynter there is no detective set to watch the Duchess. Bosola does not appear until the very end of the story, when he is hired to murder Antonio. What is so ridiculous in Webster is the position of this paid spy, who is a member of the Duchess's household for three years, and watches her producing a surreptitious family, without ever discovering who the father is. Can there be the least doubt that Webster ought to have made the brothers leave their sister unwatched until scandalous rumors reached them, that they should then have sent an agent to find out what was going on, and that, on his discovering the secret, the catastrophe should have followed like a thunder-clap? The part Webster assigns to Bosola is a glaring example of constructive inefficiency.

At last Ferdinand determines to look into matters for himself, and, by an infantile artifice, is made to discover clearly the Duchess's amour, but still without identifying her lover. As there was never any doubt of the fact of her amour, this elaborate scene leaves matters precisely where they stood two years before, except that the Duchess knows she is discovered. This being so, she determines to send Antonio out of danger, by pretending to dismiss him on a charge of peculation. Then Bosola, who has at last begun to suspect Antonio, by feigning to defend his character, lures the Duchess into a confession that he is the father of her children. These two scenes—the Duchess's dismissal of Antonio, and Bosola's discovery of her secret—are really dramatic, showing an adroit application of means to ends. And now, when at last all is out, one naturally expects the action to hurry up a little. But no such matter. Bosola, instead of trying to prevent Antonio's flight, aids and abets the Duchess in her design of following him to Ancona. It is not his fault that she does not entirely elude her brothers' vengeance. The flight to Ancona, it may be said, is part of the original story. But, once more, Webster was in no way bound to follow Paynter; and in the story there is at this point no Bosola to behave with inept inconsistency.

Presently, when he might with advantage have followed Paynter, Webster renounces his guidance. The Duchess having rejoined Antonio, Paynter provides a good reason for their parting again. They see a troop of horse approaching with the evident intention of capturing them; and, as they cannot both escape, the Duchess urges Antonio, who is well mounted, to ride off with their eldest son, she herself, as she fondly believes, having nothing to fear from her brothers. This plausible ground for their separation is ignored by Webster.

We now come to the act—the Fourth—which has earned for Webster the reputation of a superb tragic poet. Antonio has escaped to Milan, and the Duchess is back in Amalfi, where Ferdinand favors her with a visit. Alleging that he has "rashly made a solemn vow never to see her again," he begs her to receive him in the dark. Then, affecting to "seal his peace with her," he thrusts upon her a dead man's hand. She at first receives it as his, remarking

You are very cold:
I fear you are not well after your travel

—and then cries "Ha! lights!—O, horrible!" Is the invention of this
ghastly practical joke—for it is Webster's: he did not find it in his
original—is it a thing to be admired, and to earn its inventor a place
only a little below Aeschylus and Shakespeare? I submit that any mor-
bid-minded schoolboy could have conceived it, and that the humblest
melodramatist of to-day would not dare to affront his transpontine audiences by asking them to applaud such a grisly absurdity.

Next the ingenious Ferdinand draws a curtain, and shows the Duchess wax figures of Antonio and their son, apparently lying dead. It is
manifestly impossible that Ferdinand can have secured portraits in wax
of the man and child; yet the Duchess takes the figures for reality, and
is duly horrified. It would have been infinitely easier, safer and more
dramatic to have lied to her in words. This waxen lie is the device of a
dramatist whose imagination works on the level of a Tussaud Chamber
of Horrors.

Then comes the famous and much-admired Dance of Madmen which
Ferdinand provides to enliven his sister's last moments. It is preluded
by the Duchess's beautiful speech to Cariola:

> I'll tell thee a miracle:
> I am not mad yet, to my cause of sorrow:
> The heaven o'er my head seems made of molten brass,
> The earth of flaming sulphur, yet I am not mad.
> I am acquainted with sad misery
> As the tann'd galley-slave is with his oar.

That Webster was a poet no one denies; yet this same poet, on the
next page, treats us to a song by a madman, sung "to a dismal kind of
music" says the stage-direction, of which this is the first verse:

> O, let us howl some heavy note,
> Some deadly, dogged howl,
> Sounding as from the threatening throat
> Of beasts and fatal fowl!

When the eight madmen have gone through their frigid antics and
talked their dismal nonsense, Bosola enters disguised as an Old Man, an-
nounces himself as a tomb-maker, and talks a great deal of fantastic
stuff "fit for a charnel," as the Duchess aptly observes. Then enter "Executioners, with a coffin, cords, and a bell," who proceed to strangle, on
the open stage, first the Duchess, and then the struggling, shrieking,
biting and scratching Cariola. From the modern editions it would seem
that they also strangle in sight of the audience the Duchess's two young
children. But when we read the original quarto, in the light of our
better knowledge of the structure of the Elizabethan stage, we see that

the children were strangled behind the scenes, and their bodies revealed by the drawing of a curtain.

Now it was of this scene in especial that Charles Lamb wrote:

> What are "Luke's iron crown," the brazen bull of Perillus, Procrustes' bed, to the waxen images which counterfeit death, the wild masque of madmen, the tomb-maker, the bellman, the living person's dirge, the mortification by degrees! To move a horror skilfully, to touch a soul to the quick, to lay upon fear as much as it can bear, to wean and weary a life till it is ready to drop, and then step in with mortal instruments to take its last forfeit; this only a Webster can do. Writers of an inferior genius may "upon horror's head horrors accumulate"; but they cannot do this. They mistake quantity for quality, they "terrify babes with painted devils," but they know not how a soul is capable of being moved; their terrors want dignity, their affrightments are without decorum.

I yield to no one in my love and reverence for Charles Lamb; but I cannot conceal my conviction that a more topsy-turvy criticism than this was never penned. Others, forsooth, "mistake quantity for quality"! If ever any man did so it was surely Webster. We may be wrong in thinking his quality very poor, but there can be no mistake as to his quantity being excessive. Other people's terrors "want dignity"—is Ferdinand's trick with the dead man's hand a dignified terror? Other people's "affrightments are without decorum"—is the masque of lunatics a decorous affrightment? Is all this calculated "to touch a soul to the quick"? If ever there was a crude and unblushing appeal to the physical nerves, this is surely it.

With the death of the Duchess, the interest of the play is over; for Antonio is admittedly a shadowy character as to whose fate we are very indifferent; and though we are willing enough to see Ferdinand, the Cardinal and Bosola punished, we could quite well dispense with that gratification. Webster, however, is not the man to leave any of his *dramatis personae* alive if he can help it; so, as Rupert Brooke says, he kills off his criminals "with various confusions and in various horror." The Cardinal's irrelevant mistress, Julia, dies of kissing a poisoned book—a favorite incident with the Elizabethans. The Cardinal himself is killed by Bosola, his attendants disregarding his cries for help, because he has told them that he will very likely imitate the ravings of his mad brother, and no one must pay any attention—a piece of imbecile ingenuity such as tyros in playwriting are apt to plume themselves upon. Bosola kills Antonio by mistake, and Ferdinand and Bosola kill each other. There is scarcely room on the stage for all the corpses; which is perhaps the reason why, in the Phoenix revival, Ferdinand stands on his head to die, and waves his legs in the air.

All the editors of *The Duchess of Malfi* make a bald statement that Lope de Vega treated the same theme; but I have seen no comparison between Lope's play and Webster's. It is not one of his well-known works; but after some trouble I discovered it at the British Museum and read it. The Spanish and the English conventions are so very different that minute comparison is hardly possible. *El Mayordomo de la Duquesa de Amalfi* is not so much a play as an opera, full of brilliant bravura passages. But Lope's play is a much less barbarous product than Webster's; and I have no hesitation in saying that his catastrophe is immeasurably superior. It is highly concentrated, and, though rather too horrible for modern tastes, intensely dramatic. The Duchess and Antonio have parted, as in the original story. Then Ferdinand (here called Julio) succeeds in persuading them that he is reconciled to their union, and that Antonio has only to return to Amalfi for all to end happily. We see Antonio pass from one room into another in which he expects to find the Duchess; and then we see the Duchess hurrying to meet Antonio; but when the curtains are opened behind which she expects to find him, what she does find is a table set forth with three salvers on which are the heads of Antonio and their two children. This plunge from the height of joyful expectancy to the abyss of anguish and despair is incalculably more dramatic than Webster's laborious piling up of artificial horrors. After a pathetic outburst of lamentation, the Duchess, who has been poisoned, falls dead.

Lope's conclusion, too, is humanized by the fact that the Duke of Amalfi, the Duchess's legitimate son, whom Webster only mentions in passing, warmly espouses his mother's cause. I should be glad to know what the admirers of Webster's Duchess make of the fact that she never gives a word or a thought to the offspring of her first marriage.

This attempt to apply rational canons of dramatic construction to an Elizabethan "masterpiece" will doubtless be regarded in many quarters as little less than sacrilegious. The time is surely approaching, however, when the criticism of the Elizabethans will no longer be left to scholars who know nothing of the theater (Lamb's own plays show clearly how little he understood it), and who have not the elementary power of distinguishing between poetic and specifically dramatic merit.

Spatial Structure in *The Duchess of Malfi*

by Una Ellis-Fermor

The Jacobeans, better than most other poetic dramatists, afford us instances of another highly interesting structural characteristic, that of a play which contains two types of experience simultaneously throughout its extent and thus offers its form to be considered simultaneously in two aspects. One type of experience is primarily concerned with the subject matter as a chronological record of event and proceeding from this we arrive at an aspect of form described most naturally in terms of plot, story and the causal connection of event. The other experience is spatial instead of temporal and it regards the play as a grouping of moods, characters, forms of diction or of prosody and looks for form in the interrelations of these. The first may be, and indeed generally is, affected by extra-aesthetic knowledge,[1] the second is an entirely aesthetic experience having reference solely to the individual drama under consideration. Obviously the two experiences may either fuse into a single aesthetic experience or remain in some degree dissociated. For the moment, the point I should like to make is that drama does in certain cases, and they are relatively frequent in the Jacobean period, afford this second form, which can be considered apart from that composed of the series of events that make the plot.[2]

This can perhaps be made clearer by reference to the art in which the distinction is habitually made, that of painting. There the two experiences derived from what are often spoken of as the subject matter and the "body" or plastic, are habitually distinguished in criticism whether or not they co-operate in the actual picture discussed. We can think, that is, of what the picture represents, illustrates or means; we can think alternatively of the form which grows out of the relation of the masses, and we may, if we are able and when we are familiar

"*Spatial Structure in* The Duchess of Malfi" (*Editor's Title*) *by Una Ellis-Fermor. From* The Jacobean Drama: An Interpretation (*New York: Random House, Inc., 1958; London: Methuen & Co., Ltd., 1958, [4th ed., revised-1st ed., 1936]*) , *pp. 38-44. Copyright 1936 by Una Ellis-Fermor. Reprinted by permission of the publishers.*

[1] As in the case of *The White Devil.*

[2] As has been pointed out, in the case of Shakespeare, by Mr. Wilson Knight. See especially *The Wheel of Fire* (1930), Chap. I.

with the picture, have an aesthetic experience which fuses the two. In the case of pictures or of plays which are able to do this, the experience derived from extra-aesthetic knowledge tends to drop out, and in a completely realized work of art such as the *Duchess of Malfi* it will, I think, have been transmuted so that the "story" gradually ceases to have importance, very much as does the element of illustration in a picture. It would be absurd to suggest that in a play there is naturally a complete divorce of these two elements. "Of course," as Mr. L. A. Reid says, "the painter is interested in the expressiveness of visual *forms*. But he is interested in their *expressiveness*. The forms are "significant." And what does a human face express more definitely than human character." [3] That is very nearly the position of character in drama. An examination of *The Duchess of Malfi* (as a privately read drama, for the moment, rather than as a theater production) will, I think, illustrate this point, and will serve to suggest, as Mr. Wilson Knight for instance has led us to deduce in the case of Shakespeare, that in drama of certain kinds an aesthetic experience akin to that of the plastic in painting can be recognized. As he himself says, however, of his own somewhat different distinction between the spatial and temporal aspects of the play, "It is evident that my two principles thus firmly divided in analysis are no more than provisional abstractions from the poetic unity." [4]

But because literature, like music, must be revealed in time, there will be a definite succession in time of these effects just as the outward form is revealed by a definite recounting in time of the events. It would be enough in considering some plays to map these spatial relations statically and in the less highly developed cases this probably marks fairly their achievement in the direction of inner forms. [5] But for the highly evolved works of art this is not enough and the inner form only reveals itself fully when it is perceived as a progression of such relations.

In drawing together our impressions of the *Duchess of Malfi* we probably notice first of all certain related rhythms of the characters, such as would be given by our first impression of the potentially moving masses of a picture. The eye is carried first to the figure of the Duchess because of the clear luminous quality with which it is invested

---

[3] L. A. Reid: *A Study in Aesthetics* (1931), Chap. XII, *Competition and its Types* (p. 321).

[4] Wilson Knight: *The Wheel of Fire* (1930), Chap. I, p. 5. See also the subsequent argument and the volume, *passim*.

[5] It is often the case in straightforward comedy of character combined with intrigue, for example. I think, to choose a few instances at random, that it will be found true of *Gammer Gurton's Needle*, *A Mad World, my Masters*, *The Good-Natured Man* and similar cases.

(mainly through the imagery connected with her) and next but almost simultaneously to the group made of Ferdinand and Bosola, the tension and implied rapidity and confusion of movement in Ferdinand contrasting and throwing up the ease and limpidity of the portrayal of the area occupied by the Duchess, in which we next notice the subsidiary figures of Antonio and Delio. Midway between the two, drawn a little back, but constituting a point of balance to which the eye tends more and more to return, is the Cardinal, whose function in the play seems like that of some center of immobility in a picture; his stillness throws up the movements, whether disjointed or co-ordinated, of the other figures of the drama; the hardness and impenetrableness of his texture emphasizes the sentient life in them and is emphasized by it.

But this mapping of the static relations of the figures cannot be carried further without underestimating the subtlety of the play, for that depends rather upon something like the sequence of relations in a musical composition. Not only are the characters so grouped that the mind passes with increasing aesthetic satisfaction from one figure or group of figures to another, always led by the contrasts and re-affirmations which the playwright himself has indicated, the masculine toughness of Julia against the more slender but no less enduring quality of the Duchess, each emphasized in a death speech which is, as it were, a point of light bringing out the contrast while yet emphasizing the fundamental community of color in both minds. It is not only in this delicate relating of mood and quality, a relating which spreads over the whole play and whose effect could be analyzed in immense detail, it is not only in this that Webster shows his supreme understanding of such form as was germane to his purpose, such form as, without slavery to verisimilitude, could mirror immediately his thought. The whole of this subtly articulated group produces also in the course of the play an ordered progression of moods as though the lighting of a picture should be replaced by another lighting and that again by a third, while all the time the value of the relations between the masses and of the relations between the colors remained undiminished or even increased in strength while they themselves and the very relations between them changed and were transmuted. Thus neither the characters, nor the mood which each calls up in the reader, nor the relations between the groups, are the same at the end of the play as they were at the beginning. What is perhaps more important, from somewhere in the fifth act (about the opening of the third scene) these things cease to be in themselves significant; the figures remain and the play continues apparently in order that some final aesthetic deduction as to the values in the preceding parts may be drawn in the course of the experience of that act. What is the nature of this detached and relatively abstract aesthetic experience I am not yet sure, though it is clear that it occurs in the same way in both of Webster's last acts and in a similar way in some of Ford's. As to the way in which it appears or the process by which it is brought about, we may, I think, say a little more. The action, after the murder of Julia and the final regrouping of Bosola and the Cardinal, is practically predetermined; each of the deaths that follow is intended by one character or another capable of carrying out his intention, and, though the event does not fall precisely as it was planned, the result corresponds with our expectation. This, combined with the brooding, prophetic cloud in which the moods of one after another of the characters are wrapped, serves to free us from speculation as to what will happen and simultaneously the increasing concentration of Webster's interest in the reflections of the characters and their imagery withdraws a great part of our attention from the question of how it will happen. From that moment the playwright is free to develop the concluding movement of his play mainly in terms of the inner form, leaving the outer form to wind itself off mechanically. From the entry, therefore, of Ferdinand in Scene iv, "Strangling is a very quiet death," we find our interest concentrated more and more on the speech rhythms not only in individual lines, but in increasingly long related passages which now take over the interpretation of the material of event and character and add in this way our final understanding of the relations which gave it its inner form. Imagery, therefore, and reflective comment, Webster's usual means of suggesting the existence of this inner form throughout the play, now fall into subsidiary relation to this dominating factor of verbal music, which thus becomes the final and most significant mode of expression. The rhythms become more and more packed with Webster's characteristic qualities; the thick groupings of double-stressed feet, the heavy, slow movements of the lines which seem to gather into themselves and roll back again rhythms like the intoxicating beat of a tom-tom, beyond the everyday experience of human speech; these characteristics so divert and dominate the lines that, without violent resistance, they could not be spoken naturalistically and nothing remains for the reader but to submit to this increasing volume of significant sound and for the actor but to accept an intonation which often runs across the apparent meaning of the words or the necessities of the story. After the crash and turmoil of the fighting in which Ferdinand is killed, there is a sudden silence which can only be fitly rendered as such a pause would be by the conductor of an orchestra. It is broken slowly by the voice of the dying Cardinal, "Thou hast thy payment too?" and upon Bosola's reply come in again the hurrying lords, the impetuousness half-hushed now in horror. From this moment the musical movement transcends everything else. From the clear, long-drawn tonic of Bosola's

"Revenge for the Duchess of Malfi murdered" it is a compact sequence, broken for a moment by Pescara's everyday tones, but lifted immediately after to its climax. In the hush before the great final passage Malatesta's question comes slow and still:

> Thou wretched thing of blood,
> How came *Antonio* by his death?

and then—we can almost see the conductor's baton—the long-drawn pause and the slow, almost inaudible beginnings of Bosola's last speech, gradually gathering volume until it sinks again on the last line. Hard upon this comes the almost matter-of-fact, realist movement of Delio's epilogue, which ends, as only the great artists dare to end, upon the simplest of major harmonies.

> *Mal.* O sir, you come too late.
> *Delio.* I heard so, and
>   Was arm'd for 't ere I came: Let us make noble use
>   Of this great ruine; and joyne all our force
>   To establish this yong hopefull Gentleman
>   In 's mother's right. These wretched eminent things
>   Leave no more fame behind 'em than should one
>   Fall in a frost, and leave his print in snow—
>   As soone as the sun shines, it ever melts,
>   Both forme and matter: I have ever thought
>   Nature doth nothing so great, for great men
>   As when she's pleased to make them Lords of truth:
>   *Integrity of life, is fame's best friend,*
>   *Which noblely beyond Death, shall crowne the end.*

And this interpretation—concerning which the rhythm of the lines appears to give no choice—is utterly alien to any plausible stage representation. Considered from the point of view of psychological probability, Malatesta's question could not, as the movement demands, drop slowly into the silence; it would come quickly, promptly, the voice of a soldier taking charge of the position. In fact, it would not be the inefficient Malatesta who would ask the question at all; it is quite alien to his character. He happens to be the only performer free at the moment. Nor could Bosola's speech be spoken (in an English theater of Webster's day or ours[6]) with that almost inaudible faintness which the

---

[6] This would, I think, be possible in a French theater, especially a *théâtre intime* of small proportions and in certain of the Little theaters of England, America and Germany. But it seems, as far as it is possible to judge, impossible to produce in a large public theater without disregarding the prosodic indications I have suggested above.

implied musical notation demands. These things Webster left to his producer to solve and it was enough for a practical theater man that he left a more or less naturalistic presentation possible as well. But behind, indeed in contradiction to, the stage effects, he gave us the unmistakable indications of his own interpretation of the values of the play. These, by the end of the play, have almost completely separated from and transcended the chronological record of events or plot.

Fate and Chance in *The Duchess of Malfi*

by Muriel C. Bradbrook

In the second prison scene of *The Duchess of Malfi* there is a significant echo of the most terrible chapter in the Pentateuch, which seems hitherto not to have been recognized:

> I'll tell thee a miracle—
> I am not mad yet, to my cause of sorrow.
> Th' heaven ore my head, seemes made of molten brasse
> The earth of flaming sulphure yet I am not mad: (IV. ii. 25-8)

> But it shal come to passe if thou wilt not hearken unto the voyce of the Lord thy God, to observe to do all his Commandments and his Statutes which I command thee this day, that all these curses shall come upon thee and overtake thee.
> Cursed shalt thou be in the city and cursed shalt thou be in the field.
> Cursed shall be thy basket and thy store.
> Cursed shall be the fruit of thy body and the fruit of thy land. . . .
> And the heaven that is over thy head shall be brasse, and the earth that is under thee shal be yron. . . .

> So that thou shalt be mad for the sight of thine eyes which thou shalt see.
>
> *(Book of Deuteronomy, xxviii. 15-18, 23, 34)*[1]

The Duchess both compares and distinguishes her plight from that depicted in the curse of Mount Ebal: the earth under her feet is not iron but the flaming sulphur of hell; nor is she granted the oblivion of madness. But the original context is not irrelevant, as it is in so many of Webster's borrowings.

The power of a curse, though it may be related to a coherent belief, is more usually superstitious, i.e. it involves the supernatural as part

---

"Fate and Chance in The Duchess of Malfi*"* by Muriel C. Bradbrook. From "Two Notes Upon Webster" in The Modern Language Review, XLII (1947), 281-91. Copyright © 1947 by Modern Humanities Research Association. Reprinted by permission of the Modern Humanities Research Association.

[1] From the Authorized Version (1611) which appeared some two years before the play.

of the free energy, the undirected power of the universe. The horror of
Webster's play depends upon a powerful sense of the supernatural combined with a scepticism far deeper than that of professed rebels like
Marlowe. An intense capacity for feeling and suffering, within a clue-
less intellectual maze, springs from the deepened insight into character
which was Webster's greatest strength as a dramatist.[2] Fear of the
unseen and unapprehended encompasses all his characters: the
world to come is even darker than the midnight in which all his
greater scenes are laid.[3]

> In what a shadow, or deepe pit of darknesse,
> Doth (womanish, and fearfull) mankind live.   (v. v. 125-6)

The curse which falls upon the Duchess of Malfi is potent but
undefinable, like the whole atmosphere of the supernatural in this
play. The malice of her brothers is the immediate cause of her sufferings, but even as the hidden vindictiveness of the Cardinal sur-
passes the savagery of Ferdinand, it is a power beyond these two
which the Duchess curses first and foremost: no less than the "stars"
themselves, which include in themselves or by their influence the
whole material universe, the frame of things entire.

> I could curse the Starres . . .
> And those three smyling seasons of the yeere
> Into a Russian winter: nay the world
> To its first Chaos.   (IV. i. 113-19)

To which Bosola, the instrument of Fate, opposes an implacable
calm:

> Look you, the Starres shine still.   (IV. i. 120)

The Duchess's reply, though in itself a bitter jest, implies the con-
tagious nature of a curse: "Oh, but you must remember, my curse
hath a great way to goe" and runs on without a stop into the curse
of the plague itself which she wishes on her brothers.

There are roughly five types of curse:[4] curses upon wrongdoers,

[2] Cf. Professor Hardin Craig, *The Enchanted Glass* (Oxford University Press, 1936),
pp. 226-7.
[3] The bedroom scene, the two prison scenes and the final scene are all night scenes.
Cf. that chapter of *Job* which Bosola quotes elsewhere, "the land of darknes and the
shadow of death. A land of darknes, as darknes it selfe, and of the shadow of
death, without any order, and where the light is as darknes" (*The Book of Job*,
x. 21-2).
[4] This classification is my own. I have been unable to find any systematic study of
the variety of curse beyond Ernest Crawley's little book, *Oath, Curse and Blessing*
(Watts, 1934).

either by the sufferer (imprecation) or the Church (excommunication); curses as adjunct to an oath; malignant cursing of the innocent by witches and sorcerers; hereditary curses (blights) upon a family—usually an extension of cursing in the first sense; and general curses upon specific acts, by whomsoever committed, which are a form of primitive legislation and of which the Jewish curse pronounced by the Levites from Mount Ebal is a powerful example.

The curse which the Duchess lays on her brothers invokes the powers of God and is a religious imprecation. Such a curse is the last weapon left to the helpless and oppressed, and was frequently used in Elizabethan tragedy, notably by Titus in *Titus Andronicus,* by Anne and other victims in *King Richard III,* by Constance in *King John,* and pre-eminently by Timon and Lear. The power of such a curse was greatest in a parent or king, in whose outraged authority God saw an image of His own. Cornelia, therefore, when she utters her twofold curse upon Vittoria and Brachiano, is armed with this double power of authority and wrong.[5]

In the earlier scene where she first recognizes the doom which is upon her, the Duchess realizes that the hereditary curse lies upon her children, and says

> I intend, since they were born accurs'd;
> Cursses shall be their first language.   (III. v. 137-8)

Indeed a curse, irrespective of the guilt or innocence of the individual, may well be hereditary in "the royall blood of *Arragon,* and *Castile*" to which the Duchess and her brothers belong, the physical tie which twinned her with Ferdinand and which is the only cause of the tragedy.

> Damne her, that body of hers,
> While that my blood ran pure in't, was more worth
> Than that which thou wouldst comfort, (call'd a soule)
>   (IV. i. 146-8)

he cries to Bosola, but the pure blood of her royal descent which it is her crime to have contaminated carried, as all would know, the curse of that madness which later overtook Ferdinand himself.[6]

The curses which Ferdinand so freely vents are spoken in a transport of rage, but the solemn act of banishment performed by the Cardinal and the States of Ancona, which must have been spectacu-

---

[5] *The White Divel,* I. ii. 288-93. Cornelia kneels to utter this curse, as was commonly done. In the first act of *The Divel's Law Case,* the mother kneels and curses her daughter the same way: and the daughter is aghast (I. ii. 112-14).

[6] The story of Juana the Mad, sister of Katherine of Aragon, must have been known to the audience, and that of the children of Philip II.

larly one of the highlights of the play, has the full weight of civil and ecclesiastical authority behind it. That this is misused authority the pilgrims who act as chorus to the scene bear witness; but the splendors of the shrine of Our Lady of Loretto had been used previously in drama as a background to Machiavellian "policy." [7]

In his earlier play Webster had used a good deal of merely furious cursing: Vittoria, Brachiano and Isabella (in her playacting) are more violent than deadly,[8] the politicians do not curse, and Cornelia herself at the end says to Flamineo:

> The God of Heaven forgive thee. Do'st not wonder
> I pray for thee? Ile tell thee whats the reason,
> I have scarce breath to number twentie minutes,
> Ide not spend that in cursing.   (*The White Divel,* v. ii. 52-5)

In *The Duchess of Malfi* the most potent curses are "not loud but deep." A vow spoken with imprecation may constitute a curse: such is Brachiano's vow "by his wedding ring" not to lie with Isabella, which she calls a "cursed vow." Ferdinand's vow never to see his sister more, which he makes the opportunity for a cruel deception, rebounds upon himself—as an unjust vow was likely to do—for it is the sight of her supposed dead face which unnerves him and awakes the madness in him.

It is Ferdinand who refers most frequently to the practices of the Black Art. Thrice does he accuse the Duchess herself of witchcraft (i. i. 344-6, ii. v. 1, iii. ii. 165), but when Bosola suggests that she is the victim of sorcery, he scorns the idea:

> Do you thinke that hearbes, or charmes
> Can force the will? Some trialls have bin made
> In this foolish practise; but the ingredients
> Were lenative poysons, such as are of force
> To make the patient mad. . . .
> The witch-craft lies in her rancke blood.[9]   (iii. i. 88-94)

Nevertheless, part of her torment was that she was watched, i.e. prevented from sleeping, a recognized method of dealing with those who were themselves witches. In presenting the wax figures of Antonio and

---

[7] By Chapman, *Byron's Tragedy,* i. ii. 78-82.

[8] Vittoria, *The White Divel,* iii. ii. 286-91, iv. ii. 125-40; Brachiano, ii. i. 190-4, iv. ii. 43-9; Isabella, ii. i. 245-54. Primitive curses often depend on a formula, and on being spoken in due posture, at a favorable hour of day.

[9] When Byron says that he has been bewitched by La Fin into committing treason, his accusers point out that witchcraft cannot affect the will, which, being one of the faculties of the rational soul—the others were reason and memory—could not be enforced.

his children "appearing as if they were dead," Ferdinand practices directly upon her life by a method analogous, as the Duchess herself recognizes, to the most famous and deadly of charms.

> It wastes me more,
> Than were't my picture, fashion'd out of wax,
> Stucke with a magicall needle, and then buried
> In some fowle dung-hill   (IV. i. 73-6)

At the same time Ferdinand leaves with her a dead man's hand bearing a ring, with the words "Bury the print of it in your heart." The Duchess, discovering it, cries:

> What witch-craft does he practise, that he hath left
> A dead-man's hand here?   (IV. i. 65-6)

This is a powerful charm which was also used in the cure of madness,[10] but which as the "Hand of Glory" or *main de gloire* was an essential ingredient in the more deadly practices of the Black Art. The ring, which the Duchess is meant to see as Antonio's, is her own wedding ring which the Cardinal had violently torn from her before the shrine of Our Lady of Loretto: and a wedding ring was itself a sacred object possessed of virtuous powers.

These horrible properties do in fact so benumb the Duchess that she feels to live is "the greatest torture soules feele in hell" (IV. i. 82) and the servant who wishes her long life has pronounced a most "horrible curse" upon her (IV. i. 110). The executioners "pull downe Heaven upon" her (IV. ii. 238), and Hell opens before her murderers, both Bosola (IV. ii. 269) and Ferdinand. The curse of her blood lies upon them and cries for vengeance (IV. ii. 78-80). The sight of her dead face enacts her silent revenge upon them. It was generally believed that in the presence of a murderer the wounds of a corpse would bleed, the eyes might open and fix him with a blighting look, or the dead hand might point to him in denunciation. The effect on Ferdinand is to awake remorse: he denounces the murder and his tool Bosola, saying that the deed is registered in hell (IV. ii. 327). This is perhaps an echo of Othello to the dead Desdemona: "That look of thine will hurl my soul from heaven. . . ."

The form of madness which overtakes him, lycanthropy, was recognized as a diabolic possession:

> The devill, knowing the constitution of men, and the particular diseases whereunto they are inclined, takes the vantage of some and secondeth the nature of the disease by the concurrence of his own delusion, thereby corrupting the imagination and working in the mind a strong

[10] G. L. Kittredge, *Witchcraft in Old and New England* (Harvard, 1929), p. 142.

persuasion that they are become that which in truth they are not. This
is apparent in that disease, which is termed *Lycanthropia,* where some,
having their brains distempred with melancholy, have verily thought
themselves to be wolves and so have behaved themselves. . . . For God
in his just judgment may suffer some men to be bewitched by the devill,
that to their conceite they may seeme to be like brute beasts, though in
a deede they remaine the true men still.

William Perkins, *A Discourse of the Damned art of Witchcraft . . .*
(*Works,* 1618, III, 611)[11]

In the last act Bosola and Antonio are haunted by the Duchess,
whilst Ferdinand and the Cardinal are haunted by devils, and death
overtakes all four. The curse which has involved the whole family is
worked out.

> These wretched eminent things
> Leave no more fame behind 'em, then should one
> Fall in a frost, and leave his print in snow—
> As soone as the sun shines, it ever melts,
> Both forme, and matter   (v. v. 138-42)

The influence of the stars is the divine method of governing the world
as Sir Kenelm Digby points out in a passage which, though some
twenty years later than the date of *The Duchess of Malfi,* may be cited
as a typical statement of the general belief:

. . . no accident can be so bad in this life but that the celestial bodies
have power to change it to good . . . not chance but the heavens and
stars govern the world which are the only books of fate: whose secret
characters and influences but few, divinely inspired, can read in the true
sense that their Creator gave them.

This in no way impugns the doctrine of free will, for God having
framed the world upon the strife and counterpoise of contraries, such
as hot and cold, poisons and antidotes, summer and winter, to human
souls, His highest work, He gave

an entire liberty together with a constrained necessity which no way
hinder or impeach each other.

The highest faculty of knowledge is the contemplation of the Creator
and this the human soul is free to accept or reject, subject only to
God's unconstraining foreknowledge. This inner freedom being
granted, in the course of the outer world God governs not by direct
and miraculous intervention, but arranges that

---

[11] It is perhaps fair to add that King James in *Daemonologie* denied the supernatural origin of this disease. Bodin, *Demonomanie* (1580), accepts it.

inferiors should be subaltern to and guided by their superiors: the heavens then and stars, being so in respect of us, not only in place but in dignity, duration, in quantity, in quality and in purity of substance . . . must of necessity be allowed by us to be the causes of all contingent accidents and the authors of our fortunes and actions whereby the liberty of the will doth not immediately and expressly repugn and wrestle against the disposition of the heavens . . . since to meaner lights we by daily experience attribute the ominous presages of the deaths of kings, of revolutions and of empires, wars, pestilence, famine, dearths, and such other effects, let us without difficulty acknowledge a nobler operation in these glorious bodies that are the efficient causes of the other: and having admitted them for causes, you will grant that who hath the knowledge of their natures may, by calculating their motions for time to come, prognosticate their effects.[12]

By their foreknowledge, prognosticators could attempt to avert evil influences, and strengthen good ones—to rule the stars. This, however, was considered impious,[13] and although the casting of horoscopes was common enough, Antonio's one attempt to read the stars brings disaster. The *Life* of Cardano makes plain the real discomforts of star-readers. Bosola, it would appear, does not believe in the power of the prognosticators; though he does not go so far, with Shakespeare's Edmund, as to deny the power of the stars themselves:

> *Bosola.* Tis rumour'd she hath had three bastards, but
> By whom, we may go read i' th' Starres.
> *Ferd.* Why some
> Hold opinion, all things are written there.
> *Bosola.* Yes, if we could find Spectacles to read them.   (III. i. 72-6)

The most extensive statement of this doctrine comes in the central scene of Chapman's *Conspiracy of Byron,* a play to which *The Duchess of Malfi* shows particular indebtedness. The astrologer himself begins by foreseeing some danger to himself, which he feels unable to avert:

> O the strange difference 'twixt us and the stars;
> They work with inclinations strong and fatal,
> And nothing know; and we know all their working
> And nought can do, or nothing can prevent!   (III. iii. 6-8)

When he has read the fatal horoscope of Byron in which a Caput Algol prognosticates that the Duke is to lose his head, Byron curses

---

[12] *Private Memoirs of Sir Kenelm Digby,* ed. Sir. N. H. Nicholas (1827), pp. 127-32.

[13] Cf. Professor Hardin Craig, *op. cit.,* p. 6. He quotes *Paradise Lost,* VIII, 83-4: "Heaven is for thee too high | To know what passes there. Be lowly wise." G. Cardano cast the horoscope of Christ.

him, and defies the stars, because as a rational soul he is of nobler
substance than they.

> I am a nobler substance than the stars,
> And shall the baser overrule the better? . . .
> I have a will and faculties of choice
> To do, or not to do: and reason why
> I do, or not do this: the stars have none:
> They know not why they shine, more than this taper,
> Nor how they work, nor what: I'll change my course,
> I'll piecemeal pull the frame of all my thoughts,
> And cast my will into another mould. . . .
> [I'll] kick at fate. Be free, all worthy spirits,
> And stretch yourselves for greatness and for height,
> Untruss your slaveries: you have height enough
> Beneath this steep heaven to use all your reaches;
> Tis too far off to let you, or respect you.   (III. iii. 109-18, 130-4)

However, like other tragic heroes the Duke rushes on his ruin, disregarding all the omens and warnings which he receives, and in the end,
his friends can only pray that he

>   ope his breast and arms,
> To all the storms Necessity can breathe,
> And burst them all with his embraced death
>   (*Byron's Tragedy*, v. iii. 212-14)

which he does in that fine image which is also echoed by the Duchess,
that the body is

> A slave bound face to face with Death till death.   (v. vi. 38)

But Byron's triumphant defiance of death is no stoic acceptance of its
pangs. He succeeds finally, in facing it—only that, and no more. He
accepts the fact that a life as passionate and heroic as his own must be
extinguished, but he cannot tolerate the circumstances: he, a single
man, defies the "kingdom's doom" (v. iv. 217), and his death, like his
life, is a clash of opposites, "vice and virtue, corruption and eternesse"
mixed (v. iv. 190-1). In this he is a true microcosm or little world of
warring elements.

He cites, only to reject them, the conventional Stoic maxims, not
because he does not believe them, but because he will not accept them
as platitudes from the lips of the bishop who attends him.

>   Talk of knowledge!
> It serves for inward use.   (v. iv. 50-1)

Chapman's perfect stoics, Clermont D'Ambois and Cato, whose tempers are so settled that no calamity can disturb them, are something less heroic, as well as less human. Though they claim to accept their fate "freely," "with a man's applause," the impression they give is rather one of indifference.[14] The Duchess, who submits to the chastisement of Heaven, though the instruments are tyrannous (III. i. 90-5), has a natural courage and nobility of spirit that rises at the scent of danger. When she turns, expecting to see her husband, and sees her brother behind her, her first words are:

<blockquote>'Tis welcome   (III. ii. 77)</blockquote>

And again when she sees the troop of armed men making towards her across country:

<blockquote>O, they are very welcome: (III. v. 111)</blockquote>

Bosola says that she seems "rather to welcome the end of misery" than shun it (IV. i. 5-6), and at the very nadir of her hopes, when she has reached the calm at the center of the whirlpool, the Duchess, equating herself, like Edgar, with the "lowest and most dejected thing" of nature, discovers the anaesthesia that lies beyond.

<blockquote>
I am acquainted with sad misery,
As the tan'd galley slave is with his Oare,
Necessity makes me suffer constantly,
And custome makes it easie.   (IV. ii. 29-32)
</blockquote>

Her misery is *sad* because it is settled and established, because it is adult and mature, and because it is massive and heavy, like the oar, a physical burden.[15] *Necessity* may stand either for the situation or for the stern goddess, *saeva Necessitas,* who has created it: and *constantly* means both continuously, or incessantly, or steadfastly and heroically (which is the older sense). There are thus two meanings combined in this passage: the Duchess is inured to the pain which she cannot escape, but she has also learnt to suffer, and acquired strength from her sufferings. The first meaning is supported by the image of the galley slave: yet after all, it was only the strongest who could survive in the galleys.[16]

---

[14] *Revenge of Bussy D'Ambois,* III. iv. 70, IV. i. 149; cf. I. iv. 132, IV. v. 6.

[15] For these various meanings of *sad, necessity* and *constantly,* see *New English Dictionary* s.v.

[16] In *Believe as You List,* a play which once or twice echoes Webster, the deposed King Antiochus, whose stoic fortitude defies imprisonment and torture, is literally sent to the galleys, and appears as a galley slave in Act V.

When, finally, Bosola brings in the coffin with the words "may it arrive welcome . . ." the Duchess turns to face the last present of her Princely brothers with the words:

> I have so much obedience, in my blood,
> I wish it in ther veines to do them good.   (IV. ii. 168-9)

This does not of course mean that she is obediently accepting death, but that her blood (i.e. her passions, all that Ferdinand meant by "her rancke blood") is now entirely obedient to her will, and therefore she is not physically terrified, or transported with physical rage as was Byron: she wishes that the choleric blood of her brothers were as obedient as hers. She is Duchess of Malfi still.

To doubt the power of the stars was perhaps atheistic and impious,[17] but on the other hand, to accept it would seem to leave Man, for all practical purposes, dependent on the second causes, and his fate to be, in Bosola's phrase, the star's tennis balls. This phrase was used also, however, with a significant variant—Fortune's tennis.[18] Fortune, or "blind chance" was one of the commonest figures in Elizabethan pageantry, emblem books and devices. With her wheel, upon which humanity was bound, "her rolling restless stone" [19] and her blinded eyes, she might be presented in a favorable aspect as Chance or Opportunity, in which case she had a long forelock, to be seized by the active and aspiring man; but more frequently she personified the "turning and inconstant and mutability and variation" of unregulated accident, which calls attention to itself only when the accident is unfavorable. It is in this aspect that Kent defies her when he is set in the stocks by Regan:

> Fortune, goodnight,
> Smile, once more turne thy wheele
> > *(King Lear,* II. ii. 179-80)[20]

Blind Fortune plays so large a role in *The Duchess of Malfi* that her influence may almost be thought to challenge that of the stars. It is the name under which the Duchess gives herself to Antonio, perhaps in recollection of the courtly habit by which ladies assumed such

---

[17] Lipsius, *De Constantia,* lib. 4, restated the classic argument for reconciling stellar influence and man's freewill, originally popularized in Boethius.

[18] "The Starres tennys balls," v. iv. 63. *Fortune's Tennis* was the title of a play by Dekker, now lost: and also of an anonymous fragment dated *c.* 1600 (Chambers, *Elizabethan Stage,* IV, 14).

[19] Fluellen's description of Fortune, *Henry V,* III. vi. 20 ff.

[20] And—how typically—Cordelia: "For thee, oppressed King am I cast downe, | Myself could else outfrowne false Fortunes frowne."

allegorical roles. Later Delio, fearing that he is betrayed, cries

> how fearfully
> Shewes his ambition now, (unfortunate Fortune)!   (II. iv. 105-6)

And if the dreadful horoscope which does in fact betray Antonio illustrates the malignancy of the stars, the accident which makes him
drop it in Bosola's path is a freak of chance. This accident has often
been censured as undramatic, a flaw in Webster's construction; it is
on the contrary, eminently dramatic, as the recent production of this
play made clear: it is precisely the kind of odd, unpredictable coincidence which, when events are wrought up to a sufficiently high pitch,
can almost be counted on to occur. In the late war, half the casualties
resulted from some such accident—and half the miraculous escapes.
Some one just happened to be called away before the bomb fell, or
just happened to have gone into the cellar. It is of course only in
times of violence that such accidents mean the difference between life
and death.

The Duchess greets those who have come to apprehend her with a
defiance of Fortune:

> O, they are very welcome;
> When Fortunes wheel is overcharg'd with Princes,
> The waight makes it move swift. I would have my ruine
> Be sudden.   (III. v. 111-14)

And in prison she thinks that her tragedy is terrible enough to un-
muffle blind Fortune (IV. ii. 37-8). Antonio goes to his fatal interview
with the same contempt of what Fortune can do:

> Though in our miseries, Fortune have a part,
> Yet, in our noble suffrings, she hath none—
> Contempt of paine, that we may call our owne.   (v. iii. 70-2)

In the last act of *The Duchess of Malfi* mere ill-fortune directs the
"mistakes" by which Bosola and Antonio are killed: yet the Echo had
bid Antonio fly his *Fate* (v. iii.), and when Delio begs him not to go
to the Cardinal's that night, he replies with a bitter punning jest that
suggests a stronger power than blind Chance at work:

> Necessitie compells me[21]   (v. iii. 41)

The play is filled with little omens, such as the Duchess's dream that
her coronet of diamonds was changed to pearls, Antonio's name being

---

[21] Necessity in the sense of *poverty*, and necessity in the sense of *fate*. For another
vital play upon this word, see the words of the Duchess quoted above.

drowned in blood, the tangling of the Duchess's hair;[22] and as the
Pilgrim says, on witnessing their banishment:

> Fortune makes this conclusion generall,
> "All things do helpe th' unhappy man to fall."   (III. iv. 48-9)

The alternative views that Fate or Chance rule the world are never
set in open opposition to each other, and the omens might be interpreted as the work either of the one or the other. It is precisely this
uncertainty at the heart of the play which is the heart of its darkness:
either explanation, if it could be accepted as an explanation, would
give some relief. But the opposition of Fate and Chance was in fact a
familiar one;[23] the problem would be obvious to Webster's audience,
without any formal antithesis being propounded. The astounding
and gratifying thing is that he should have been able to resist the
temptation to state a case; it is a renunciation of which few Elizabethans were capable, and least of all perhaps his friend Chapman.
The spectator, like the Duchess, goes into a wilderness where there is
neither path nor friendly clue to be his guide. The Cardinal and
Ferdinand may die acknowledging the justice of their ends in the
highly sententious manner which was expected at the end of a Revenge play, but Bosola, to the end of his final couplet adds four mysterious words which come from a state far on the other side of despair.

> Let worthy mindes nere stagger in distrust
> To suffer death, or shame, for what is just—
> Mine is another voyage.   (V. v. 127-9)

This blank feeling of Lucretian chaos is as far removed from the
Deistic "atheism" of Marlowe as from the determinist stoicism of
Ford. Bosola, the conscience-struck and bewildered slave of greatness,
so dominates any presentation of the play that the loves and crimes
of the House of Aragon seem but a background to his tragedy. Ferdinand, the Cardinal and the Duchess are born to rule: their imperious
tempers are innate. Ferdinand draws his dagger before his sister, even
when he has no reason to suspect her of a second marriage:

---

[22] III. v. 19-21, II. iii. 59-62, III. ii. 61. Antonio says of the second, that the superstitious would call it ominous, but he believes it chance, "meere accedent."

[23] Perhaps the best example of this commonplace is the frontispiece of R. Recorde,
The Castell of Knowledge, 1556, which shows a castle with Astrology on the top: on
the left, Knowledge upholding the Sphere of Destiny, and on the right, blindfold
Ignorance holds the cord of a crank which turns the Wheel of Fortune inscribed
Quomodo scandit, corruet statim. The Motto runs: "Though spiteful Fortune turned
her wheele, | To staye the Sphere of Uranye, | Yet dooth this Sphere resist that
wheele | And fleeyth all fortunes villanye. | Though earth do honour Fortunes
balle | And bytells blinde her wheele advaunce, | The heavens to fortune are not
thralle, | These Spheres surmount al fortunes chance."

> This was my Fathers ponyard: doe you see,
> I'll'd be loth to see't look rusty, 'cause 'twas his   (I. i. 370-1)

The Duchess turns away, and almost her next words are:

> If all my royall kindred
> Lay in my way unto this marriage:
> I'll'd make them my low foote-steps.   (I. i. 382-4)

Bosola, a silent figure, listens to these high words from the Prince to whom he has already sold himself in what he recognizes as a diabolical bargain (I. i. 285-94). His sympathy for the Duchess in the discovery scene is far more deeply felt than the momentary flash of compunction which Brachiano's betrayers feel: and the shock of his final comment:

> What rests, but I reveale
> All to my Lord?   (III. ii. 374-5)

is only deepened by his self-contempt. After her capture he essays to comfort the Duchess without ever being able to defy Ferdinand who observes contemptuously:

> Thy pity is nothing of kin to thee   (IV. i. 166)

The word echoes through the latter half of the play: pity, "the miracle of pity," and having carried out the murder, Bosola retorts the word upon his master:

> But here begin your pitty   (IV. ii. 272)

Remorse works in Ferdinand as madness: the Hell which he had foreseen when he accepted Ferdinand's gold engulfs Bosola, and wakens in him the same vengeful love which in the earlier play Ludivico had felt for the wronged Duchess Isabella. It is Bosola, not Antonio, who speaks the most passionate lines in the play:

> Returne (faire soule) from darknesse, and lead mine
> Out of this sencible Hell: She's warme, she breathes:
> Upon thy pale lips I will melt my heart
> To store them with fresh colour.   (IV. ii. 368-71)

He weeps (IV. ii. 390) and later he is haunted by the memory of the scene:

> Still me thinkes the Dutchesse
> Haunts me: there, there. . . . Tis nothing but my mellancholy
>   (V. ii. 381-2)

It is as the embodiment of that blind and bewildered pity which, striking with his bitterness, occasionally rises into a general disillu-

sion, that Bosola dominates the play. His great speech on the vanity
of life, addressed to the captive Duchess in preparation for her death,
recalls in its function the great speech of the Duke to the captive and
condemned Claudio in *Measure for Measure,* but its immediate source
is the Book of Job. This speech, more than any other, epitomizes what
the play is really concerned with.

> Thou art a box of worme-seede, at best, but a salvatory of greene
> mummey: what's this flesh? a little cruded milke, phantasticall puffe-
> paste: our bodies are weaker then those paper prisons boyes use to keepe
> flies in: more contemptible: since ours is to preserve earth wormes: didst
> thou ever see a Larke in a cage? such is the soule in the body: this world
> is like her little turfe of grasse, and the Heaven ore our heades, like her
> looking glasse, onely gives us a miserable knowledge of the small compasse
> of our prison.[24]   (IV. ii. 122-31)

Webster had a delicate balance to maintain between the theatrical
and the doctrinal in this scene. There is no doubt that the "scene of
suffering" in a Senecal play included physical atrocities of a kind
which could not be paralleled in Webster: and that in the plays of
the Machiavellian villain parricide was a necessary ingredient. It was
therefore necessary, if his subject were to be brought home to his
audience, that the action should be violent. In such a case the natural
compensating impulse of the Elizabethan dramatist was to indulge in
extended monologue, such as Constance's apostrophe to Death in
King John, the "passions" of Marston's characters, or the great set
speeches of Chapman's tragic heroes. But Webster successfully steers
between this Scylla and Charybdis. The pageantry of madness and
death, the waxen figures, the disguises of Bosola all suggest that the
events are inadequate to express the nature of the sorrow in which the
Duchess is enfolded. The quality of her endurance is as far removed
from the stoic insensibility of the "Senecal man"—Feliche, Clermont
or Charlemont—as it is from the hysteric passions of Marston's Antonio. Her insensibility is the natural insensibility of extreme shock,
and it passes. Through her "sensible Hell" she moves as a human
figure, whose delicate gradations of mood show that even at the end,
it is life, vulnerable but unquenchable, which dazzles the eyes of
Ferdinand and which he (and we) mistake for death.

---

[24] "Remember I beseech thee that thou hast made me as the clay and wilt thou
bring me into dust againe? Hast thou not powred me out as milke and cruddled
me like cheese? Thou hast cloathed me with skin and flesh and hast fenced me
with bones and sinewes . . . Hast thou with him spread out the sky, which is
strong and as a molten looking glasse?" (*The Book of Job,* x, 9-11, xxxvii. 18.) The
rest of ch. x. is all highly relevant, e.g. the verses quoted on p. 211, n. 3, and also
9. 22-4. The verse directly used here by Webster seems also to be behind one of
the sonnets of G. M. Hopkins: "Bones built in me, flesh filled, blood brimmed the
curse" (*Poems,* no. 45).

A Perspective that Shows Us Hell

by Travis Bogard

In *The Duchess of Malfi* the themes of the corruption of court life and of courtly reward and punishment are continued. Antonio's description of the ideal French court with which the play opens and his dying request, "And let my Son, fly the Courts of Princes," are sufficient evidence that the themes of *The White Devil* are present in the later play. But in the second tragedy they are no longer central. *The White Devil* is intensely concerned with the Jacobean world, treating the evils which man creates—the forces of social tyranny. The drama only hints at forces more profound than those created by man, as in the overtones of such a line as Brachiano's:

> On pain of death, let no man name death to me,
> It is a word infinitely terrible—   (v. iii. 39)

There is a suggestion here of something deeper, working in secret to produce a greater horror than man can bring on himself—a natural evil which man cannot control.

The Duchess of Malfi turns the few dark hints of the sister tragedy into actuality. It brings into focus on the stage all the terrors of a dying universe. Not sudden death, but dying by slow degrees, sinking into a morass of disease and rot—this is what the human integrity must now face. The theme of social evil, which in the earlier play is called courtly reward and punishment, is still heard, but now it is only a part of a much greater whole, as when an actor playing a scene before the curtain is suddenly refocused into a much larger world of activity by the drawing of the curtain to reveal the entire stage.

As in *The White Devil*, the theme is stated early in the play. At the beginning of the second act, Bosola mocks the gull Castruchio and the old woman who, presumably, is midwife to the Duchess. In words reminiscent of the "comical satire" plays, Bosola demonstrates how

"A Perspective that Shows Us Hell" by Travis Bogard. From The Tragic Satire of John Webster *(Berkeley and Los Angeles: University of California Press, 1955), pp. 131-41. Copyright © 1955 by the Regents of the University of California. Reprinted by permission of the publisher.*

Castruchio can be taken for an eminent courtier. He then turns on the crone and mocks her for painting her face, as the formal verse satirists flayed their subjects for the same offense. Antonio has called Bosola a malcontent and a victim of a foul melancholy; and it seems, as Bosola speaks, as if the black bile rises high in his gorge, forcing him to move from disgust at the specimens before him to a general loathing of all humankind.

Having finished with Castruchio, Bosola proceeds to an analysis of the midwife's closet.

> One would suspect it for a shop of witch-craft, to find in it the fat of Serpents; spawn of Snakes, Jews' spittle, and their young children's ordures—and all these for the face: I would sooner eat a dead pigeon, taken from the soles of the feet of one sick of the plague, than kiss one of you fasting: here are two of you, whose sin of your youth is the very patrimony of the Physician, makes him renew his foot-cloth with the Spring, and change his high-pric'd courtezan with the fall of the leaf: I do wonder you do not loathe your selves—observe my meditation now:
>
> (II. i. 37)

Bosola suddenly forgets his victim and turns savagely on mankind. Webster indicates the significance of the passage with the verbal colon, "observe my meditation now," and a change from prose to verse.

> observe my meditation now:
> What thing is in this outward form of man
> To be belov'd? we account it ominous,
> If Nature do produce a Colt, or Lamb,
> A Fawn, or Goat, in any limb resembling
> A Man; and fly from't as a prodigy.
> Man stands amaz'd to see his deformity,
> In any other Creature but himself.
> But in our own flesh, though we bear diseases
> Which have their true names only ta'en from beasts,
> As the most ulcerous Wolf, and swinish Measle;
> Though we are eaten up of lice, and worms,
> And though continually we bear about us
> A rotten and dead body, we delight
> To hide it in rich tissue—all our fear,
> (Nay all our terror) is, lest our Physician
> Should put us in the ground, to be made sweet.   (II. i. 45)

The speech confronts the audience with the loathsome reality of the processes of natural decay, a subject which was barely suggested amid the social evils of *The White Devil*. In *The Duchess of Malfi*, the theme of natural evil is central to the play.

This theme, like that of courtly reward and punishment, is divided into three parts which are treated concurrently through the tragedy: first, the bestiality of man; second, the conception of the rotting body, accompanied by images of sexuality and of widespread corruption; and third, the dignity of death.

The first two aspects of the theme are, like the theme of courtly reward and punishment in the sister tragedy, satiric commonplaces, and Webster's initial treatment of the conventional material is in the tradition of formal satire. His verse is vivid and, in the passages leading to Bosola's meditation, Webster is content to let the themes reside in the images of the dialogue. Comparisons of men with animals, insects, and rapacious birds fill the first act.

> He, and his brother, are like Plum-trees (that grow crooked over standing-pools) they are rich, and o'erladen with Fruit, but none but Crows, Pies, and Caterpillars feed on them: Could I be one of their flattering Panders, I would hang on their ears like a horse-leech, till I were full, and then drop off. (I. i. 50)

> The Spring in his face, is nothing but the Engend'ring of Toads.
> (I. i. 159)

>   . . . the Law to him
> Is like a foul black cob-web, to a Spider—
> He makes it his dwelling, and a prison
> To entangle those shall feed him. (I. i. 180)

The second thematic element is presented in similar fashion. The degeneration of the body, sexuality, and less specific personal or social corruption provide images which establish at the outset the play's basic concerns.

> If too immoderate sleep be truly said
> To be an inward rust unto the soul;
> It then doth follow want of action
> Breeds all black malcontents, and their close rearing
> (Like moths in cloth) do hurt for want of wearing. (I. i. 79)

> There's no more credit to be given to th' face,
> Than to a sick man's urine, which some call
> The Physician's whore, because she cozens him. (I. i. 250)

> *Ferdinand:* A Vizor, and a Mask are whispering rooms
>   That were nev'r built for goodness: fare ye well:
>   And women like that part, which (like the Lamprey)
>   Hath nev'r a bone in't.
> *Duchess:* Fie Sir!

> *Ferdinand:* Nay,
>   I mean the Tongue: variety of Courtship . . .   (I. i. 373)

>   what's my place?
> The Provisor-ship o'th' horse? say then my corruption
> Grew out of horse-dung.   (I. i. 311)

>   a Prince's Court
> Is like a common Fountain, whence should flow
> Pure silver-drops in general: But if't chance
> Some curs'd example poison't near the head,
> "Death, and diseases through the whole land spread.   (I. i. 12)

Bosola's "meditation" synthesizes and makes explicit the first two elements of the main theme; thereafter the animal metaphor and the images of degeneration flood the dialogue. The pregnancy of the Duchess is described in terms of the corruption of the flesh. Later, Bosola again waylays the midwife, and jibes at her with allusions to sexual abnormality. During the confusion attendant upon the birth of the child, the servants spread lewd tales of a Switzer caught in the Duchess' bedroom with a pistol in his codpiece. Soon thereafter, Ferdinand and the Cardinal swear vengeance on their sister. Their words, filled with images of bestiality and degeneration, are like a summary of what has gone before.

> *Ferdinand:* Methinks I see her laughing,
>   Excellent *Hyena*—talk to me somewhat, quickly,
>   Or my imagination will carry me
>   To see her, in the shameful act of sin.
> *Cardinal:* With whom?
> *Ferdinand:* Happily, with some strong-thigh'd Bargeman;
>   Or one o'th' wood-yard, that can quoit the sledge,
>   Or toss the bar, or else some lovely Squire
>   That carries coals up, to her privy lodgings. . . .
>   Go to (Mistress)
>   'Tis not your whore's milk, that shall quench my wild-fire,
>   But your whore's blood.
> *Cardinal:* How idly shows this rage! . . . I can be angry
>   Without this rupture—there is not in nature
>   A thing, that makes man so deform'd, so beastly,
>   As doth intemperate anger.   (II. v. 52, 76)

Throughout the first part of the play Webster never ceases to emphasize these thematic metaphors, which stress vividly man's bestiality and degeneration by frank statement and vile suggestion.

But such evil was to become more than a metaphor. What to the satirists had been commonplace comparisons are turned unexpectedly into living reality, when at the end of the play the animal image is translated into action in Ferdinand's madness. Ferdinand falls victim to lycanthropy, the "melancholy humour" whereby men imagine themselves to be transformed into wolves,

> Steal forth to Church-yards in the dead of night,
> And dig dead bodies up. (v. ii. 12)

The incident was carefully planned. Ferdinand's mind, long before he becomes irrational, is dwelling on wolves. He compares the Duch-ess' voice to the howling of a wolf. Her children are "Cubs," and he says, when he views their bodies,

> The death
> Of young Wolves, is never to be pitied. (iv. ii. 274)

When Ferdinand goes mad, the image becomes actuality. The beast in man appears in its grimmest, most horrible manifestation. Ferdi-nand *is* an animal. The metaphor is interpreted literally, and pre-sented in a way unknown to the formal satirists, as reality that under-lay the cause of evil in the outward form of man. Bosola had said, "Man stands amaz'd to see his deformity, / In any other Creature but himself," and Webster expected his audience to stand amazed at this spectacle of the bestial overthrowing the human. With the animal metaphor he deliberately set the deformities of men, physical and spiritual, into relief against a world of unregulated instincts.

Images of sex, general corruption, and bodily rot, like the animal images, appeared frequently in the work of other satirists. Marston and Tourneur are full of them. Again, however, Webster did not stop with the images, but showed them in action. The scene in which Julia, the Cardinal's depraved mistress, woos Bosola to her bed is sufficient example of the realization of sexual images in the dramatic action. Its surface is strangely quiet, almost casually straightforward. But the strength and the ugliness of the episode come from its star-tling echo of the scene in which the Duchess proposes to Antonio. The Duchess had said,

> The misery of us, that are born great!—
> We are forc'd to woo, because none dare woo us: . . .
> I do here put off all vain ceremony,
> And only do appear to you a young widow
> That claims you for her husband, and like a widow,
> I use but half a blush in't. (i. i. 507, 525)

In similar words, Julia cajoles the man she wants:

> Now you'll say,
> I am wanton: This nice modesty, in Ladies
> Is but a troublesome familiar,
> That haunts them. . . . I am sudden with you—
> We that are great women of pleasure, use to cut off
> These uncertain wishes, and unquiet longings,
> And in an instant join the sweet delight
> And the pretty excuse together.   (v. ii. 176, 205)

Although the scenes are placed at opposite ends of the play, the similarity is striking. Certainly, in contrast with the beauty and health of the earlier scene, the later parallel becomes an active manifestation of the images of sexual corruption which infest the drama.

In like manner, the images of widespread social and individual corruption become more than metaphors. As in *The White Devil,* the behavior of the great princes and prelates is thoroughly dishonest. The machinations of Ferdinand and the Cardinal, the Cardinal's stealthy attempts to cover his part in the crime, the spectacle of sycophants, flatterers, intelligencers, and murderers which surround the Aragonian brothers make the images of social corruption appallingly real. As for the moral corruption of the individual, there is Bosola, whose life is a voluntary embracing of such evil.

With the images pertaining to bodily rot, Webster approaches the farthest reaches of terror. Bosola had lamented that "though continually we bear about us / A rotten and dead body, we delight / To hide it in rich tissue." In the fourth act, this aspect of the central theme is used to rouse the Duchess to the fullest assertion of her integrity. The body, he tells her, is rotten, weak, worthless.

> Thou art a box of worm-seed, at best, but a salvatory of green mummy: what's this flesh? a little crudded milk, fantastical puff-paste: our bodies are weaker than those paper prisons boys use to keep flies in: more contemptible: since ours is to preserve earth-worms.   (iv. ii. 123)

It is the ultimate degradation, the final revelation of the reality beneath the Duchess' dignified and gracious appearance. But it is this image which enables her to assert, in spite of the worthlessness of her outward form, that she is "Duchess of *Malfi* still."

In the development of the third thematic division, the dignity of death, Webster sounded the depths of the problem of evil which he had first faced in *The White Devil.* Bosola's "meditation" gives the theme preliminary statement.

> all our fear,
> (Nay all our terror) is, lest our Physician
> Should put us in the ground, to be made sweet.

Images of death are everywhere in *The Duchess of Malfi*. They all
but dominate the proposal scene. Ferdinand conjures up fantastic
ways of murdering the Duchess and her husband, and his images of
murder twine with the sexual imagery to create a horrifying effect.

> I would have their bodies
> Burnt in a coal-pit, with the ventage stopp'd,
> That their curs'd smoke might not ascend to Heaven:
> Or dip the sheets they lie in, in pitch or sulphur,
> Wrap them in't, and then light them like a match:
> Or else to boil their Bastard to a cullis,
> And give't his lecherous father, to renew
> The sin of his back.   (II. v. 87)

There are the strange, hysterical images of death the Duchess evoked
when she was confronted by the strangling cord. There is Bosola, disguised as a maker of tombs; there are the wax figures and the dead
man's hand; and there are the murders of the Duchess and the scream-
ing Cariola. In almost every scene, death makes its appearance.

The fifth act has repeatedly been criticized as an anticlimactic clut-
tering of the stage with corpses. It is true that with the death of the
Duchess in the fourth act a light goes out of the play. The heroic
story has been told. But the satiric story, the revelation of the real
condition of man's world, has not been completed. The fifth act with
its frightening development of the theme of death is essential to the
picture of the tragic world.

The fourth act shows the destruction of good by evil and the way
in which humanity can assert its integrity even in defeat. The fifth
act shows what happens in a world where good is dead and integrity
is absent. The lascivious Julia is murdered by her lover. Antonio is
killed in error by the man who sought to save him. The Cardinal is
trapped by Bosola. A servant who attempts to summon help is stabbed.
The Cardinal's screams for help rouse the lunatic Ferdinand, and in
the three-way scuffle the "wretched eminent things" are fatally
wounded. Evil turns on evil: these are the rampaging disasters that
follow the destruction of good, the full flood tide of death. The last
act of the tragedy does indeed present what William Archer called a
"butcher's bill"; but it is not without meaning.

The deaths in *The Duchess of Malfi* are different in their effect
from the slaughters in *The White Devil*. In the latter, the murders
were the working out of social evils, the product of deliberate vengeance. Francisco and Monticelso are alive at the play's end, triumphant in what they have done. With the exception of Flamineo, the
characters are in no sense resigned to their deaths. In *The Duchess of
Malfi*, however, Webster is careful to show that all the important

characters except the hysterical Cariola and the insane Ferdinand welcome death as inevitable. They seem to feel that death is not the result of man's inhumanity to man so much as a slight hastening of the processes of natural decay and a return, ultimately, to sweetness. The Cardinal asks "to be laid by, and never thought of." Bosola's soul is weary. Antonio senses that life is merely "a preparative to rest." Their words echo those of the Duchess:

> Tell my brothers,
> That I perceive death, (now I am well awake)
> Best gift is, they can give, or I can take— . . .
> Come violent death,
> Serve for *Mandragora,* to make me sleep.   (IV. ii. 229, 242)

There is terror in this death struggle of evil, but there is dignity as well, and quiet—a quiet that seems almost an answer to the tormenting problems of the world.

The "Impure Art" of John Webster

by Inga-Stina Ekeblad

The art of the Elizabethans is an impure art. . . . The aim of the Elizabethans was to attain complete realism without surrendering any of the
advantages which as artists they observed in unrealistic conventions.[1]

Obviously *The Duchess of Malfi* is an outstanding example of the
"impure art" of the Elizabethans. Here, in one play, Webster plays
over the whole gamut between firm convention and complete realism:
from the conventional dumb-show—

> *Here the Ceremony of the Cardinalls enstalment, in the habit of a
> Souldier: perform'd in delivering up his Crosse, Hat, Robes, and Ring,
> at the Shrine; and investing him with Sword, Helmet, Sheild, and Spurs:
> Then* Antonio, *the* Duchesse, *and their Children, (having presented them-
> selves at the Shrine) are (by a forme of Banishment in dumbe-shew, ex-
> pressed towards them by the Cardinall, and the State of Ancona) ban-
> ished* [2] (III. iv)—

to the would-be realistic pathos of

> I pray-thee looke thou giv'st my little boy
> Some sirrop, for his cold . . . ;   (IV. ii. 207-8)

or from the horror-show of *"the artificiall figures of* Antonio, *and his
children; appearing as if they were dead"* (IV. i. 66-67) to the realization of a character's psychological state, in such lines as Ferdinand's
much-quoted "Cover her face: Mine eyes dazell: she di'd yong"
(IV. ii. 281) or Antonio's "I have no use | To put my life to" (V. iv.
74-75).

So Webster's dramatic technique needs to be understood in relation
to the "confusion of convention and realism" which Mr. Eliot speaks

---

"The 'Impure Art' of John Webster" by Inga-Stina Ekeblad. From Review of
English Studies, IX *(1958), 253-67. Copyright 1958 by Oxford University Press. Reprinted by permission of the Clarendon Press, Oxford.*

[1] T. S. Eliot, *Selected Essays* (New York, 1950), pp. 96, 97.

[2] I quote from *The Complete Works of John Webster,* ed. F. L. Lucas (London,
1927).

of; and indeed many critics would in this "confusion" see the key to Webster's alleged failure as a dramatist. They would say that Webster's method of mixing unrealistic conventions with psychological-realistic representation leads to lack of structure in his plays as wholes.[3] It seems, in fact, to have become almost an axiom that when Webster uses conventional dramatic material—such as the various Revenge play devices—it is for show value, "for effect," and not because the progress of his dramatic action, and the meaning of the play, are vitally tied up with that convention—as they are, for example, in *The Revenger's Tragedy* or *The Atheist's Tragedy*. While Tourneur's "bony lady" is simultaneously an incentive to revenge and a tool for moralizing, the *memento mori* and center of meaning of the play, Webster's wax figures seem to have no other function than Madame Tussaud's. And while Tourneur's famous speech, "Do's the Silke-worme expend her yellow labours | For thee? . . . ," is closely dependent on, and interacts with, the skull on the stage, Webster's dramatic meaning would appear to inhere in his poetry—such as Bosola's ". . . didst thou ever see a Larke in a cage?"—irrespective of the dramatic devices employed. Is it then, only when his poetry fails to do the trick that Webster "falls back on showmanship,"[4] such as "all the apparatus of dead hands, wax images, dancing madmen and dirge-singing tomb-makers in *The Duchess of Malfi*?"[5]

Now, while recognizing that in other Elizabethans than Webster (for example Tourneur) the dramatic form is more firmly and consistently controlled by established conventions, we must, on the other hand, not blind ourselves to the richness which may inhere in the very "confusion" of convention and realism. The two can be confused; but they can also be fused. And I hope to show that Webster—though he often leaves us in confusion—does at his most intense achieve such a fusion, creating something structurally new and vital. This something, however, is very much more elusive to analysis than the more rigidly conventional structures of Tourneur, or the more clearly "realistic" structure of Middleton (as in *The Changeling*).

I wish to examine *The Duchess of Malfi*, IV, ii—the Duchess's death-scene. It is a part of the play to which no critic of Webster has been indifferent; it stirred Lamb's and Swinburne's most prostrate praise and Archer's most nauseated denunciation, and later critics have only

---

[3] Cf. M. C. Bradbrook, *Themes and Conventions of Elizabethan Tragedy* (2nd edn., Cambridge, 1952), pp. 187, 194, 211.

[4] *The Age of Shakespeare*, Pelican Guide to English Literature (London, 1955), p. 352.

[5] W. A. Edwards, "John Webster," *Scrutiny*, ii (1933), 20. Cf. also Ian Jack, "The Case of John Webster," ibid., xvi (1949), 38-43.

less ardently condemned or lauded it. Its complexity has been sensed, but hardly satisfactorily analysed.[6]

No one, I think, would deny that this scene contains Webster's most penetrating piece of character-analysis. Through language where juxtaposition of sublime and lowly suggests the tremendous tension in her mind:

> Th'heaven ore my head, seemes made of molten brasse,
> The earth of flaming sulphure, yet I am not mad:
> I am acquainted with sad misery,
> As the tan'd galley-slave is with his Oare   (iv. ii. 27-30)

we follow the Duchess's inner development towards the acceptance of her fate; till finally, though "Duchesse of *Malfy* still," she humbly kneels to welcome death. And yet, in the midst of this representation of human experience, Webster introduces a pack of howling madmen, to sing and dance and make antic speeches; and as they leave the stage, the whole apparatus of "dirge-singing tomb-makers," etc., is brought in. How are we to reconcile such apparently opposed elements? The commonly accepted answer is that this is only one more instance of Webster's constant letting us down, his constant sacrifice of unity of design, in order to achieve a maximum effect. But, in a scene which is so clearly the spiritual center of the play, which verbally—through poetic imagery—gathers together all the chief themes of the play and thus becomes a kind of fulcrum for the poetry, ought we not to devote particular attention to the dramatic technique used, before we pronounce it as grossly bad as the answer suggested above would indicate?

In fact, if we pursue the question why Webster inserted a masque of madmen in a would-be realistic representation of how the Duchess faces death, we shall find that the madmen's masque is part of a larger structural unit—a more extensive masque. Within the scene, this larger masque is being developed on a framework of "realistic" dramatic representation—the framework itself bearing an analogous relationship to the masque structure. The action of the scene is grasped only by seeing both the basic framework and the masque structure, and the progressive interaction of the two. It is this structural counterpointing of "convention" and "realism," this concentrated "impurity" of art, that gives the scene its peculiar nature; indeed, it contains the meaning of the scene.

[6] Miss Bradbrook sees this scene as largely symbolical: it represents the Duchess's Hell, or Purgatory (*Themes and Conventions*, p. 197). Miss Welsford, in *The Court Masque* (Cambridge, 1927), pp. 295-96, has some suggestive, though not very clear, comments on symbolical features in this scene.

By 1613-14, the years of the composition of *The Duchess of Malfi,*
the introduction of a masque in a play was a long-established dramatic
device. In the Revenge drama, from Kyd onwards, masques were traditionally used to commit revenging murder[7] or otherwise resolve the
plot. Furthermore, in the years around the writing of *The Duchess of
Malfi* the leading dramatists show a strong interest in the marriage-
masque—we need only think of the elaborate showpiece inserted in
The Maid's Tragedy, or the masques of *The Tempest* and *The Two
Noble Kinsmen.* During these years, any play which includes a marriage seems also almost bound to contain a marriage masque.[8]

Now, in *The Duchess of Malfi* it is the Duchess's love and death,
her marriage and murder, which are the focal points of the dramatic
action. And in IV. ii Webster has, by the very building of the scene,
juxtaposed—counterpointed—the two. He has done so by drawing on
masque coventions. To see how, and why, we must proceed to a de-
tailed analysis of the scene-structure.

The essence of the masque, throughout its history, was "the arrival
of certain persons vizored and disguised, to dance a dance or present
an offering." [9] Although the structure of the early, Tudor masque
had become overlaid with literature (especially, of course, by Ben
Jonson) and with show (by those who, like Inigo Jones, thought of
the masque primarily in terms of magnificent visual effects), the
masques inserted in Jacobean plays—if at all elaborated on—stay
close to the simpler structure of the Elizabethan masque. That structure, we may remind ourselves, is as follows:

1. Announcing and presenting of the masquers in introductory speeches
   (and songs).
2. Entry of masquers.
3. Masque dances.
4. Revels (in which the masquers "take out" and dance with members of
   the audience).
   A further contact between masquers and audience—especially common when the masque is still near to its original form: groups of dis-

---

[7] Cf. Vindice's words: "A masque is treasons licence, that build upon; | Tis mur-
ders best face when a vizard's on" (*The Revenger's Tragedy,* v. i. 196-7).

[8] The two traditions of revenging-murder masque and marriage-masque sometimes
meet. See, for example, Middleton's *Women Beware Women* (1625?), where the cu-
pids' arrows are literally deadly, and Hymen himself carries and presents a poisoned
cup.

[9] Welsford, *Court Masque,* p. 7. In discussing the masque I also draw on R. Bro-
tanek *Die englischen Maskenspiele* (Wien, 1902); P. Reyher, *Les Masques anglais*
(Paris, 1909); E. K. Chambers's chapter on "The Masque" in *The Elizabethan Stage*
(Oxford, 1923) i. 149-212; the chapter on the masque in C. H. Herford and Percy
Simpson's edition of Ben Jonson (Oxford, 1925), ii. 249-334; and Allardyce Nicoll,
Stuart Masques and the Renaissance Stage (London, 1937).

guised dancers suddenly intruding into a festive assembly—can be the presenting of gifts by the masquers to the one, or ones, to be celebrated.

5. Final song (and speeches).

These features all appear in *The Duchess of Malfi,* iv. ii.

As the scene opens, the "wild consort of Mad-men" is heard off-stage as a "hideous noyse." The verbal imagery is preparing for the consciously scenic quality of what is to come. The Duchess turns immediately from her both ominous and ironic remark,[10] "And Fortune seemes onely to have her eie-sight, | To behold my Tragedy," to the question, "How now, what noyce is that?" Here a Servant enters, to perform the function of the Announcer of the masque: "I am come to tell you, | Your brother hath entended you some sport," and the Duchess answers, by a phrase which in terms of the plot only would seem absurd—for what is her power to give or refuse entry—but which is natural when coming from someone about to be "celebrated" with a masque: "Let them come in." The arrival of the masquers in *Timon of Athens,* i. ii, may serve to show that the opening of the scene follows the traditional pattern for the reception of unexpectedly arriving masquers:

Tim. What means that trump?

Enter Servant.

Serv. Please you my lord there are certain ladies most desirous of admittance.
Tim. Ladies? What are their wills?
Serv. There comes with them a forerunner my lord which bears that office to signify their pleasures.
Tim. I pray let them be admitted.

Now the Servant in iv. ii becomes the Presenter of the masque and delivers a speech introducing each of the eight madmen-masquers:

> There's a mad Lawyer, and a secular Priest,
> A Doctor that hath forfeited his wits
> By jealousie: an Astrologian,
> That in his workes, sayd such a day o'th'moneth
> Should be the day of doome; and fayling of't,

[10] Ironic because it echoes back to the wooing-scene, where the Duchess tells Antonio "I would have you leade your Fortune by the hand | Unto your marriage bed" (i. i. 567-8). She is here thinking of the traditionally blind figure of Fortune and merely making a playful conceit. Yet unwittingly she is expressing her own blindness to the consequences of her action. And when the image is repeated in iv. ii it is to make the tragic irony explicit. Now Fortune is no longer blind, nor is the Duchess; but what they see is only suffering and death. The Fortune image is used so as to point the almost literal opening of eyes that the action has brought about. Cf. F. L. Lucas's comments on this passage.

Ran mad: an English Taylor, crais'd i'th'braine,
With the studdy of new fashion: a gentleman usher
Quite beside himselfe, with care to keepe in minde,
The number of his Ladies salutations,
Or "how do you," she employ'd him in each morning:
A Farmer too, (an excellent knave in graine)
Mad, 'cause he was hindred transportation,
And let one Broaker (that's mad) loose to these,
You'ld thinke the divell were among them.

This product of Webster's grim comico-satirical strain is, of course, in terms of realistic plot totally out of place here. Not so, however, if seen in the relevant tradition. From 1608 to 1609 practically every court masque was preceded by an antimasque, often danced by "antics": "O Sir, all de better, vor an antick-maske, de more absurd it be, and vrom de purpose, it be ever all de better." [11] In each of the earlier antimasques, the antic figures were all of a kind, and there was no attempt to differentiate them. It is in the masques performed at the Princess Elizabeth's wedding, in February 1613,[12] that individualized comic characters first appear. It is worth noting that Campion's "twelve franticks . . . all represented in sundry habits and humours" in *The Lords' Masque*—such as "the melancholicke man, full of feare, the schoole-man overcome with phantasie, the overwatched usurer . . ."—as well as Beaumont's various figures in the second antimasque of *The Masque of the Inner Temple and Gray's Inn,* are described in much the same manner as Webster's eight madmen. Webster is here working in an antimasque tradition which was to have many uses in the drama after him. We see it, for instance, in Ford's *The Lover's Melancholy* (1628), which in III. iii has a masque of the same shape as the madmen's interlude in *The Duchess of Malfi*: six different types of Melancholy are described and present themselves; their antic talk is given; and then the Dance, "after which the masquers run out in couples."

After the presentation, the masquers themselves appear—"*Enter*

[11] Vangoose in Ben Jonson's *The Masque of Augures. With the Severall Antimasques Presented on Twelfe-Night, 1622.*
[12] Three masques, by Campion, Beaumont, and Chapman respectively, were performed on the occasion. The possibility that Webster directly imitates Campion's masque of madmen has been pointed out; and John P. Cutts, "Jacobean Masque and Stage Music," *Music and Letters,* xxxv (1954), 193, suggests that "it is Robert Johnson's music which is involved in the transference . . . of the madmen's antimasque from *The Lords' Masque* to *The Dutchesse of Malfy.*" What I am concerned with here, however, is not imitation or adaptation as such, but the fact of a common tradition.

Madmen"—and one of them sings a song to what the stage directions describe as "a dismal kind of Musique." [13] Even without the music, there is plenty of dismalness in the jarring jingle of the words:

> O let us howle, some heavy note,
>   some deadly-dogged howle,
> Sounding, as from the threatning throat,
>   of beastes, and fatall fowle.

Webster's audience had the benefit of the musical setting, which, according to Mr. Cutts, "makes a vivid and forceful attempt to convey the horror of the imagery of owls, wolves and harbingers of death." The antimasquers at the court of James frequently appeared in the shape of animals;[14] and it seems that, for example, the madmen-masquers ordered for the wedding of Beatrice Joanna in *The Change-ling* were to wear animal disguises. Stage directions in *The Change-ling* tell us: *"Cries of madmen are heard within, like those of birds and beasts,"* and the explicit comments on this are:

> Sometimes they [madmen] imitate the beasts and birds,
> Singing or howling, braying, barking; all
> As their wild fancies prompt 'em.   (III. iii. 206-8)

Here, then, is another antimasque tradition drawn upon in *The Duchess of Malfi*. The bestiality of these madmen comes out chiefly in the imagery of the song:

> As Ravens, Scrich-owles, Bulls and Beares,
>   We'll bell, and bawle our parts.

But we may be helped by other madmen-antimasquers to imagine, visually and aurally, how the song, and indeed the whole interlude, was executed.

Directly after the song various madmen speak for themselves, in a series of disjointed speeches which verbally link this episode with main themes of the whole play. Images of hell-fire, of madness and bestiality (preparing, of course, for Ferdinand's lycanthropy)—to mention only the most important—are concentrated here. After the speeches follows *"the Daunce, consisting of 8. Mad-men, with musicke answerable thereunto."* It is left to us to imagine the lumbering movements and discordant tunes which this passus must have contained;

---

[13] The setting, which had been broken in two in B.M. Add. MS. 29481 and wrongly catalogued, has recently been reassembled by John P. Cutts. He ascribes it, conjecturally, to Johnson. See *Music and Letters*, xxxiii (1952), 333-4.

[14] Cf. A. H. Thorndike, "Influence of the Court-Masque on the Drama, 1608-15," *PMLA*, xv (1900), 114-20.

yet we should not forget that, though there is only a bare reference
to it in the stage directions, the dance must have been the climax of
the madmen's interlude. Now, it is not "from the purpose," but truly
meaningful, that in the center of *The Duchess of Malfi* there should
be this antic dance, accompanied by these incoherent words and discordant tunes. We know that to the Elizabethans the unity and coherence of macrocosm and microcosm alike was naturally expressed
as a dance:

> Dancing, the child of Music and of Love,
> Dancing itself, both love and harmony,
> Where all agree and all in order move,
> Dancing, the art that all arts do approve,
> The fair character of the world's consent,
> The heavn's true figure, and th'earth's ornament.[15]

And so the climactic dance would be particularly significant in the
marriage-masque, the purpose of which was to celebrate the union
brought about by the power of Love. Ben Jonson built his *Hymenaei*
(1606) round this idea,[16] and the central dance of that masque is a
"neate and curious measure," accompanied by the following chorus:

> Whilst all this *Roofe* doth ring,
> And each discording string,
> With every varied voyce,
> In Union doth reioyce.   (306-9)

The dance in *The Duchess of Malfi*, on the contrary, acts as an ideo-
graph of the *dis*-unity, the *in*-coherence, of the Duchess's world. It acts
as a visual and aural image of what the action of the play has led to,
the difference between the happiness and unity of the wooing-scene,
imaged as the most perfect movement and melody:

> *Ant.* And may our sweet affections, (like the Sphears)
>   Be still in motion.
> *Duch.* Quickning, and make
>   The like soft Musique.   (I. i. 551-4)

and this scene where the Duchess herself has found that

> . . . nothing but noyce, and folly
> Can keepe me in my right wits.   (IV. ii. 6-7)

---

[15] Sir John Davies, *Orchestra*, ll. 666-71.
[16] There is an admirable discussion of the theme of Union in *Hymenaei* in D. J.
Gordon's "*Hymenaei*: Ben Jonson's Masque of Union," *Journal of the Warburg and
Courtauld Institutes*, viii (1945), 107-45. See esp. pp. 118-19.

By now it should be possible to say that the madmen's masque is
not just "Bedlam-broke-loose," as Archer, and with him many, would
have it. Nor do we need to excuse this interlude, as has been done, by
saying that Webster is not alone in it; that there are plenty of madmen in Elizabethan drama, and Webster's Bedlam stuff is as good as
any. Such an excuse does not save the scene, as a piece of dramatic art,
from damnation. But we are beginning to see the masque as peculiarly
functional in the play. We have seen its connexions with antimasque
conventions; now we must see how it is related to the events that are
represented on the stage.

In fact, there are reasons to believe that in this masque there is a
nucleus of folk tradition, the bearing of which on the action of the
play justifies the inclusion of the masque.

The widowhood of the Duchess is much stressed throughout the
play—from the brothers' interview with her in the very first scene,
around the motto, "Marry? they are most luxurious, | Will wed twice"
(I. i. 325-6). It is well known that objections to second marriages were
still strong at the beginning of the seventeenth century. We need go
no farther than Webster's own *Characters,* "A Vertuous Widdow" and
"An Ordinarie Widdow," [17] to get a notion of how strong they were.
Early in 1613 Chapman's satiric comedy *The Widow's Tears* (1605-6),
in which the "luxury" of two widows provided the plot, had had a
successful revival. The general attitude to widows' marriages was to
see them as "but a kind of lawful adultery, like usury permitted by
the law, not approved; that to wed a second was no better than to
cuckold the first." [18] And in Webster's source, Painter's translation of
Belleforest's story of the Duchess of Malfi, the Duchess is an *exem-
plum horrendum* to all women contemplating a second marriage:

> You see the miserable discourse of a Princesse loue, that was not very
> wyse, and of a Gentleman that had forgotten his estate, which ought to
> serue for a lookinge Glasse to them which be ouer hardy in makinge
> Enterprises, and doe not measure their Ability wyth the greatnesse of
> their Attemptes . . . foreseeing their ruine to be example for all pos-
> terity. . . .[19]

Webster's Duchess, newly widowed, marries again, and marries a man
in degree far below her—in fact one of her servants. Those are the
facts on which the plot of the play hinges; they comprise her double
"crime." But they also explain the point of the mental torture which,

---

[17] *Works,* ed. Lucas, iv. 38-39.
[18] *The Widow's Tears,* II. iv. 28-31 (in Chapman's *Comedies,* ed. T. M. Parrott,
London, 1911).
[19] William Painter, *The Palace of Pleasure,* ed. J. Jacobs (London, 1890), iii. 43.

in the coming of the madmen, Ferdinand has devised for his sister.[20]
For the madmen's interlude—such as we know it from Webster's stage
directions, and such as we divine it from the sung and spoken words
—is strikingly similar to a kind of *ludus,* one of the predecessors of
the masque proper, namely the *charivari.*

Du Cange defines *charivarium* thus: "Ludus turpis tinnitibus &
clamoribus variis, quibus illudunt iis, qui ad secundas convolant nup-
tias," and *O.E.D.* refers to Bayle's *Dictionnaire*: "A Charivari, or Mock
Music, given to a Woman that was married again immediately after
the death of her husband." The *charivari* as such was a French *ludus,*
or marriage-baiting custom, dating from the latter part of the Middle
Ages,[21] "originally common after all weddings, then directed at un-
popular or unequal matches as a form of public censure." [22] But the
practice which the word stands for was not limited to France. English
folk-customs and folk-drama knew the equivalent of the French
charivari[23]—indeed a descendant of it was still known when Hardy
put his skimmington-ride into *The Mayor of Casterbridge*. In the
early seventeenth century a widow in an English village, marrying
one of her late husband's servants, might well be visited by a band of
ruffians, showing their disapproval through clamour and antic dances.
Often we can trace the antimasque of a courtly masque back to village
ludi. Clearly the connexion between the grotesque dances of antimasques and various popular celebrations was, as Miss Welsford says,
"still felt, if not understood, in the seventeenth century" (*Court
Masques,* p. 29). And so I do not think it too far-fetched to assume
that the spectators at the Globe and the Blackfriars would have seen

[20] One meaning of the device is, of course, to drive the Duchess mad, the irony of
the scene being that it has exactly the opposite effect: it leads to terrifying clearness
of vision and composure of mind in the Duchess. See Ferdinand's motivation in
IV. i. 151-6: "And ('cause she'll needes be mad) I am resolv'd . . ." But this still
does not explain why the scene was given just the form it has.

[21] The most famous *charivari* of all is the one at the French court on 29 January
1393. A wedding was taking place between "un jeune chevalier de Vermandois" and
"une des damoiselles de la reine," who was a widow. Disguised as "hommes
sauvages," King Charles VI and five of his lords suddenly entered the hall of the
festivities, making queer gestures, uttering horrible wolfish cries, and performing an
antic dance. (Cf. Welsford, *Court Masque,* p. 44). In the end the masquers caught
fire; and though the King himself survived, he never quite recovered from the shock.
See Froissart's account in *Collection des Chroniques Nationales Françaises . . . ,*
ed. J. A. Buchon (Paris, 1825), xiii. 140-9, particularly Buchon's note, p. 142: "Le
moine anonyme de St. Denis dit que 'C'étoit une coutume pratiquée en divers lieux
de la France, de faire impunément mille folies *au mariage des femmes veuves* et
d'emprunter avec des habits extravagants la liberté de dire des vilenies au mari et à
l'épousée.' " (My italics.)

[22] Funk and Wagnall, *Standard Dictionary of Folklore, Mythology and Legend*
(New York, 1949), i. 212.

[23] See E. K. Chambers, *The Medieval Stage* (Oxford, 1903), i. 393.

in the "clamoribus variis" of Webster's madmen a kind of *charivari*
put on to "mock" the Duchess for her remarriage. They would then
have seen a meaning in Ferdinand's (and Webster's) device which totally escapes us when we see it as just one Bedlam episode among
many. For, if seen as related to the *charivari* tradition, the madmen's
masque becomes a contrivance of cruel irony on the part of Ferdinand: in a sense, the Duchess is here being given her belated wedding
entertainment. The Duchess is of "royall blood," and the wedding
of such an elevated person would have had to be celebrated with some
show allegorically bearing on the occasion. The year 1613, because of
the spectacular celebrations of the Princess Elizabeth's wedding, was,
above all years in the period, a year of marriage festivities. So the
audience would be particularly prepared to respond to the masque-
features of this Webster scene. And in that response would be the
realization of the dissimilarities of this masque from such masques as
did honor to the Princess and her Count Palatine, or the one Prospero
put on for Miranda. The Duchess's masque, as far as we have followed it, is all antimasque, all a grotesque mockery; but that is not
in itself the point. It is the cruel twist of this mockery, as the madmen's interlude turns out to be merely the antimasque prelude to a
kind of main masque, which strikes home.

Traditionally, after the masquers had danced "their own measure,"
they would be ready to "take out" members of the audience to dance.
It is this feature—the involving of the spectators in the proceedings—
which more than anything else distinguishes the masque as an art
form from the drama. And now the Duchess is indeed "taken out."
For directly upon the madmen's "own measure," Bosola, masqued
"like an old man," enters, and his "invitation," or summons, to the
Duchess is as conclusive as could be: "I am come to make thy tombe."
The Duchess has for a while been as much a passive spectator as anyone in the audience. Now, with a sudden change, she takes part in
what is happening. Bosola's disguise is like that of the traditional
masque image of Time;[24] and his appearance, while again focusing
our attention on the Duchess, turns the mock wedding-masque into
what reminds us of a Dance of Death. The text of this "dance" is
Bosola's words:

> Thou art a box of worme-seede, at best, but a salvatory of greene mum-
> mey: what's this flesh? a little cruded milke, phantasticall puffe-paste: our
> bodies are weaker then those paper prisons boyes use to keepe flies in:
> more contemptible: since ours is to preserve earth-wormes. . . .

[24] Cf. for example Time in Jonson's masque *Time Vindicated;* or Queen Elizabeth's coronation, when in a pageant "issued one personage, whose name was Tyme,
apparayelled as an olde man, with a scythe in his hand . . ." (J. Nichols, *The Prog-
resses of Queen Elizabeth* [London, 1823], i. 50).

From the point of view merely of plot this is a rather extravagant way of saying: "Like all men, you are a worthless creature," or something of the kind. But we see now that this speech is as much fed with meaning by the masque structure around it as is Tourneur's skull-speech by the presence of the *memento mori*. Webster's practical joke is not as spectacular as Tourneur's, and there is none of the grotesque fun of the "bony lady" in it; but it has some of the effect of Mutability entering into an Epithalamium, or of the skeleton Death joining the masque-dancers at the Jedburgh Abbey marriage-feast.[25] In the lines just quoted there is all the medieval sense of the perishable nature of all things, and this sense deepens as Bosola's focus widens:

> . . . didst thou ever see a Larke in a cage? such is the soule in the body: this world is like her little turfe of grasse, and the Heaven ore our heades, like her looking glasse, onely gives us a miserable knowledge of the small compasse of our prison.

There is a pointed consistency in the movement of thought, through associatively linked images,[26] from the nothingness of the Duchess's body to the despicableness of all flesh, to the plight of the soul in the body and of man in the universe—the correspondence between microcosm and macrocosm enabling Webster to move from one to the other in the last image. All that remains is to be absolute for death.

But the end of the masque is not yet reached. In the course of Bosola's and the Duchess's dialogue, horrible life is given to the masque convention of presenting gifts:

> Here is a present from your Princely brothers,
> And may it arrive wel-come, for it brings
> Last benefit, last sorrow.

The gifts are "a Coffin, Cords, and a Bell," presented by the Executioner. One is reminded of a passage in *The White Devil* where Brachiano, who is about to be strangled—also for a love-crime—is told,

---

[25] Alexander III of Scotland in 1285 married Joleta, daughter of the Count de Dreux. At their marriage-feast in Jedburgh Abbey, "while a band of maskers danced before the king and queen, Death in the form of a skeleton appeared in their midst and struck terror into spectators and performers alike" (P. Hume Brown, *History of Scotland* [Cambridge, 1902], i. 128-9). Cf. R. Withington, *English Pageantry* (Cambridge, Mass., 1918-20), i. 103.

[26] The box containing worm-seed (the pun on the two senses of "anthelmintic medicine" and "seed producing maggots" should be noticed, for in the sense of "medicine" the image is parallel to the subsequent "salvatory of greene mummey") becomes the paper prison with flies in it, the flimsiness of which was prepared for by the intervening "puffe-paste." The paper prison becomes the birdcage (which image has an extra layer of meaning because of its connection with the actual dramatic situation of the imprisoned Duchess). Each image derives from, but adds to and develops, a preceding image.

"This is a true-love knot | Sent from the Duke of Florence" (v. iii. 175-6). The parallelism is such that it is tempting to see in the earlier image the seed of an idea worked out more fully in *The Duchess of Malfi*.[27]

By this time we are ready for a change of guise in Bosola. He becomes "the common Bell-man" (who used to ring his bell for the condemned in Newgate on the night before their execution), and accompanied by the bell he sings his dirge: "Hearke, now every thing is still." The situation has turned like that threatened by the King in *Philaster*, v. iii.:

> I'll provide
> A masque shall make your Hymen turn his saffron
> Into a sullen coat, and sing sad requiems
> To your departing souls.

The dirge would answer to the concluding song of the masque; and it is here part and conclusion of the Duchess's masque. In fact, through the death-imagery of Bosola's song, we hear epithalamic echoes. The invocation,

> The Schritch-Owle, and the whistler shrill,
> Call upon our Dame, aloud,

refers, of course, to the harbinger of death so often mentioned in Elizabethan-Jacobean drama and poetry. But it also stands out as the very reverse of the traditional epithalamic theme of averting evil in the shape of birds[28]—as in Spenser's *Epithalamion*, 345-6:

> Let not the shriech Oule, nor the Storke be heard:
> Nor the night Rauen that still deadly yels,

or the last stanza of the marriage-song in *The Two Noble Kinsmen*, I. i:

> The crow, the slanderous cuckoo, nor
> The boding raven, nor chough hoar,
> Nor chattering pie,
> May on our bridehouse perch or sing,
> Or with them any discord bring,
> But from it fly.

---

[27] Cf. also the notion of masque in the last scene of *The White Devil*: Lodovico and Gasparo, "disguised," entering to murder Flamineo and Vittoria, introduce themselves ironically: "We have brought you a Maske" (v. vi. 170).

[28] See J. A. S. McPeek, *Catullus in Strange and Distant Britain* (Harvard, 1939), ch. vii.

Further, the Duchess is bidden to prepare herself:

> Strew your haire, with powders sweete:
> Don cleane linnen, bath your feete.

Preparation for death, this is; and the strewing of her hair could be taken as a penitential act, or simply as referring to the new fashion[29] —a cruel echo of her happy chatting in the bedchamber scene, just before disaster descends:

> Doth not the colour of my haire 'gin to change?
> When I waxe gray, I shall have all the Court
> Powder their haire, with Arras, to be like me.   (III. ii. 66-68)

But one may also hear an echo of Ben Jonson's *Hymenaei* where the "personated Bride" has her haire "flowing and loose, *sprinckled with grey*" (my italics)[30]—an idea which was to be taken up by Donne in the fourth stanza of his *Epithalamion* on the Earl of Somerset's wedding on 26 December 1613, to be made the basis of a witty conceit:

> Pouder thy Radiant haire,
> Which if without such ashes thou would'st weare,
> Thou which to all which come to looke upon,
> Art meant for Phoebus, would'st be Phaeton.

So the Duchess's preparations for the "laying out" of her dead body have cruel reminiscences of those connected with the dressing of the bride. And, finally, the end and climax of the dirge,

> 'Tis now full tide, 'tweene night, and day,
> End your groane, and come away,

strongly suggests the traditional exhortation at the end of the epithalamium, referring to the impatiently awaited night of the bridal bed: Catullus's lines "sed abit dies: | perge, ne remorare" (*Carmen,* lxi. 195-6) and their echo through practically every Elizabethan-Jacobean epithalamium, as—to give only one example—the final lines in Campion's *The Lords' Masque*:

> No longer wrong the night
> Of her Hymenean right,
> A thousand Cupids call away,
> Fearing the approaching day;

[29] Powdering the hair was just coming into fashion in England at this time (F. L. Lucas in *Works,* i. 255).

[30] That Jonson had most likely misinterpreted his source-books and made a mistake when he described the Roman bride as having her hair strewn with grey does not alter the argument (see my note on *Hymenaei, N. & Q.,* cci [1956], 510-11).

> The cocks already crow:
> Dance then and go!

And so the Duchess goes, not to an ardent bridegroom, but to "violent death." [31] It is the culminating irony of the scene.

There is clearly a close kinship between iv. ii and the wooing-scene of Act I. While the death-scene is interwoven with marriage-allusions, Death is very much there in the scene where the marriage *per verba de presenti* takes place. We hear, for instance, of the Duchess's will (playing, of course, on the two senses of "testament" and "carnal desire"), of winding-sheets, and of a kiss which is a *Quietus est;* of the "figure cut in Allablaster Kneeles at my husbands tombe," and of a heart which is "so dead a peece of flesh." There is, however, one crucial difference between the two scenes. In the wooing-scene, the counterpointing of marriage and death is entirely verbal: it is through "uncomical puns" and apparently irrelevant images that sinister associations are fused with the dramatic situation. In iv. ii, on the other hand, Webster has used the very building of the scene to express something of that typically Jacobean paradox which is contained in the two senses of the word "die." The masque elements in the Duchess's death-scene, then, are truly functional. Unlike, say, the masque in *The Maid's Tragedy,* which is a self-contained piece of theater (it is justified in the play as a whole by acting as an ironic foil to the actual wedding-night which follows), the masque in *The Duchess of Malfi* gathers into itself all the essential conflicts of the play. And it

---

[31] It need hardly be said that the parallel death-bed/bridal-bed is often drawn on in the drama of these years. The most spectacular instance is perhaps in *The Maid's Tragedy,* ii. i, where the deserted Aspatia helps to put Evadne to bed, the two women being played off against each other as "bed" against "bier." It was such exquisite horror that was inherited from the Jacobeans by Beddoes—see, for example, *Death's Test Book,* iv. iii. 230-57 (ed. H. W. Donner, London, 1950), where Athulf sings a song intended to be simultaneously his own dirge and his beloved's epithalamium:

> A cypress-bough, and a rose-wreath sweet,
> A wedding-robe, and a winding-sheet,
> A bridal-bed and a bier.
>
> .   .   .   .   .
>
> Death and Hymen both are here.

But one might note that the parallel, or contrast, could also be used in the most matter-of-fact manner:

> Lift up thy modest head,
> Great and fair bride; and as a well-taught soul
> Calls not for Death, nor doth controul
> Death when he comes, come thou unto this bed.

(Sir Henry Goodere, "Epithalamion of the Princess' Marriage," 1613; in *English Epithalamies,* ed. R. H. Case, London, 1896.)

does so on all levels: from the pure plot conflict between the Duchess and her brothers, involving questions of revenge and persecution, to the deep thematic clashes of love and death, man and Fate, which much of the poetry of the play is nourished by.

So Act IV, scene ii of *The Duchess of Malfi* gives an insight into Webster's "impure art." The scene as a whole neither fits into a realistic scheme of cause and effect or psychological motivation, nor does it consistently embody convention. It balances between those two alternatives. It is a precarious balance, and at other points we see Webster losing it. But in this scene he holds the tension between the two and draws strength from both sides—the kind of strength which tempts one to suggest that Webster's art is most "impure" at the centers of meaning in his plays; that his peculiar skill, not only as a dramatic poet but as a poetic dramatist, lay in the ability to utilize the very impurity of his art.

But when, finally, we try to see how Webster holds the balance between convention and realism, we seem to find that it is by poetic means: within the scene, the masque is related to the "realistic" dramatic representation of what happens, in the manner of a poetic analogy. That is, the Duchess' marriage, leading to her murder, is like a marriage-masque turned into a masque of Death. The two chief structural components of the scene are: (1) the plot situation—the Duchess imprisoned and put to death, because she has remarried, and (2) the *charivari*-like antimasque of madmen, developing into a masque of Death. In pursuing the interconnection between these two, we have come to see that they are best understood as two halves of one metaphor, certainly "yoked by violence together," but in the end naturally coming together, to give the full meaning of the scene. Conventional masque elements—such as Webster's original audience would have known from other plays—have helped to give Webster a structure on which to build up the most pregnant irony. The irony is there in the basic analogy between the represented human situation and the masque. It is clinched at individual points, when the analogy is most forcible—that is, at each new stage in the masque. And the irony culminates when the two parts of the analogy become interchangeable: the Duchess becomes "involved" in the masque, and her fate becomes one with the progress of the masque. Also, as in any effective metaphor, the implications reach beyond the immediate situation: In Bosola's worm-seed speech not only the Duchess but—in the manner of the *Danse Macabre*—all flesh and all things are involved. What Webster wanted to say here he could say in no other way. What he does say we can understand only by grasping the technique of the scene.

Moral Vision in *The Duchess of Malfi*

by Robert Ornstein

Because the *Duchess* appeared only a year or so after *The White Devil* it is dangerous to speak of the "development" of Webster's tragic art. Mr. Lucas thinks the *Duchess* a weaker play; Clifford Leech finds in it evidence of declining artistic powers.[1] I am convinced only that it is a much more mature play than *The White Devil*—the work of a dramatist who now sees life more clearly, more steadily, and more compassionately. It is not so much the expression of a personal, nihilistic disgust with life as a relatively detached study of the moral cowardice that robs life of meaning. Significantly enough, there are no glorious villains like Lodovico in the *Duchess*; the triumph and defeat of the emancipated will no longer hold the center of the stage. Evil still has a heroic facade but the facade crumbles eventually to reveal madness and womanish cowardice; the sheer bestiality of criminal desire, emphasized continually by animal imagery, assumes a graphic reality in Ferdinand's lycanthropy. Innocence is still defenseless against the onslaught of Machiavellian violence. Yet only the defenseless victim, the Duchess, has the strength to endure—the cardinal and redeeming virtue in Webster's tragic universe—and her self-possession in the face of death is a spiritual victory rather than a glorious defeat. Whereas the greatest moments in *The White Devil* are gestures of amoral defiance, the greatest moments in the *Duchess* are the moral discoveries at the close of the fourth act, which make the bloody catastrophe seem anticlimactic.

This is not to say that Webster turned didacticist in his second tragedy. We falsify his conception of character when we try to judge the Duchess by the socially unreal, pietistic standard expressed in the "character" of a "a vertuous Widdow."[2] Only Ferdinand and the Cardinal speak of the sin of marrying twice and they do not convince

---

"Moral Vision in The Duchess of Malfi" (*Editor's title*) *by Robert Ornstein. From* "The Duchess of Malfi" *in* The Moral Vision of Jacobean Tragedy (*Madison, Wis.: University of Wisconsin Press, 1960), pp. 140-48. Copyright © 1960 by the Regents of the University of Wisconsin. Reprinted by permission of the publisher.*

[1] *"The Revenger's Tragedy* and the Morality Tradition," *Scrutiny*, VI (March 1938), 402-22.

[2] T. S. Eliot, "Tourneur," *Elizabethan Essays*, p. 128.

us that the Duchess should be condemned as unfaithful to a nameless, dead husband, who is mentioned casually in passing. Nor do they convince us that she earns her torments by breaking the laws of social decorum. Her marriage to a man unworthy of her is a disastrous mistake, yet one she never regrets and which she redeems by the beauty and selflessness of her devotion. Moreover, it is not the marriage itself which is shameful but the moral compromise involved in hiding it. Deeply religious before her death, the Duchess sees her agony as heaven's scourge; but Ferdinand and Bosola, her "judges" and executioners, declare her innocent. If she is to serve as a cautionary example we must assume that had she not married she would have been safe from the animality of her brothers—as safe perhaps as Othello would have been had he chosen Iago instead of Cassio as his lieutenant.

The moralist teaches men how to avoid catastrophe; Webster is concerned only with how they accept it. The moralist explains the justice of men's falls; Webster does not reassure us that measure for measure is the law of existence. Armed with the doctrine of free will the moralist cannot believe in fatality; but in the hideous mist of error that enshrouds Webster's characters, no man can be called master of his fate, and no choice is clear until circumstances force men's decisions. Webster dramatizes the mystery of the irrational will without moralistic gloss. He offers no simple explanation of why Antonio, who is called a brave soldier, always chooses a coward's way or why Bosola obeys his baser instincts. If critics emphasize the irrationality of Ferdinand's motives rather than the Cardinal's, it is because the Cardinal does not attempt to explain his goals, while Ferdinand calls attention to the nightmarish confusion of his mind. Even as Goneril and Regan have no reason to torture Lear, so Ferdinand has no reason to torture his sister, unless a frenzied egomania is "reason" enough.

But for all the references to Fortune in the *Duchess*, Webster's characters are not the playthings of a capricious goddess. Nor are they like the heroic characters of *The White Devil* swept blindly to their graves. For the unreflecting villains of Webster's first tragedy there is no hope of redemption, no chance of moral illumination before their deaths. For Bosola, Antonio, and the others the redemptive moment is possible; the moral opportunity is real and within their grasp. They have the chance to protect, spare, or rescue the woman who is the center of their lives. Some form of moral awareness comes to all of them (even to the Cardinal), and when they awaken too late from the sordid dreams of their past they despair, not of life itself[3] but of

---

[3] See *"The Atheist's Tragedy* and Renaissance Naturalism," *Studies in Philology*, LI (April 1954), 194-207.

their contemptible selves. For Antonio and Bosola the burden of self-knowledge is almost as terrible as it is for Ferdinand. Even though it gives them the strength to try to change their lives, it warps their actions as they move through death-in-life towards the grave.

In Antonio and Bosola we confront again, but with deeper understanding, the paralysis of will that committed Flamineo to a career which he knew was hopeless. We see now that it is not conscience which makes cowards of us all but a hunger for personal safety; we discover with Bosola that security is the suburb of Hell. In *The White Devil* only the pious were deluded by false securities; in the *Duchess*, however, those who seem to see the world most clearly are most deeply infatuated with nonexistent safeties. "Realism" is itself an illusion that robs men of the strength to accomplish their purposes.

On the surface Antonio and Bosola are moral opposites, one a loyal, virtuous servant, the other a despicable Machiavellian intelligencer. Bosola decries an age in which virtue is its own reward; Antonio boasts that he has "long serv'd vertue,/ And nev'r tane wages of her." Bosola is chosen to be Ferdinand's informer because Antonio is incorruptible—the "worthy," the "good man." When Antonio sets out to face the Cardinal, Delio exclaims, "Your owne vertue save you," but neither Antonio's honesty nor Bosola's policy secure them against their fates. And it is hardly an accident that they cause each other's death, for in life they were brothers under the skin, men who committed spiritual suicide before a sword-thrust ended their miserable lives.

Like Flamineo, Bosola is a malcontent, embittered by experience, and hungry for the security which advancement will afford. He lacks Flamineo's high-spirited wit but he is capable of true moral feeling, and although he can for a time relish his Machiavellian successes he is finally appalled by Ferdinand's insane revenge upon the Duchess. He would like to be "honest" in Antonio's way, but he knows himself and the world too well to try, and he can never escape the self-pitying anger of the "neglected" man. Early in the play he complains to his former master, the Cardinal:

> I have done you better service then to be slighted thus: miserable age,
> where onely the reward of doing well, is the doing of it!   (I. i. 32-34)

This ironic mockery of the ideal of virtue for its own sake is completed by the knowledge that Bosola's "good service" was murder. He recognizes only two ways of "doing well": either through profitless virtue or by profitable villainy. Thus when Ferdinand offers gold, he immediately asks:

So:
What followes? (Never raind such showres as these
Without thunderbolts i'th taile of them;) whose throat must I cut?

(I. i. 264-66)

He is tempted to refuse these corrupting gifts which would take him
"to hell," but unable to refuse he accepts his servitude in a pathetic
and revealing speech:

I would have you curse your selfe now, that your bounty
(Which makes men truly noble) ere should make
Me a villaine: oh, that to avoid ingratitude
For the good deed you have done me, I must doe
All the ill man can invent: Thus the Divell
Candies all sinnes o'er: and what Heaven termes vild,
That names he complementall.

(I. i. 295-301)

If Bosola does not yet have a conscience, he has certain moral needs.
He is genuinely outraged, it seems, by the hypocrisy and sanctimony
that delight the more deeply cynical Flamineo. And unlike Flamineo,
who serves to be free from service, he seeks to give meaning to his life
by loyal service—first to Ferdinand and then to Antonio. Assuming,
however, that moral service is impossible when great men are not
noble, he chooses a cutthroat's honor, a scrupulous adherence to the
bargain that gold seals and reward justifies. Too poor to look up to
heaven, he asks Antonio's leave "to be honest in any phrase, in any
complement whatsoever—shall I confesse my selfe to you? I look no
higher then I can reach . . ." (II. i. 90-92). This is the "realist's"
defeatist credo. Too cowardly to aspire to virtue, Bosola will dare any
criminal act before he dares to assume control over his own destiny.
So long as he believes that he will save himself by loyal service, he remains true to his politic code. But when Ferdinand rewards him with
a curse for murdering the Duchess, his cynicism disintegrates into
plaintive questioning:

Let me know
Wherefore I should be thus neglected? sir,
I serv'd your tyranny: and rather strove,
To satisfie your selfe, then all the world;
And though I loath'd the evill, yet I lov'd
You that did councell it: and rather sought
To appeare a true servant, then an honest man.

(IV. ii. 353-59)

Bosola is the feudal liege man brought up to Jacobean date; he is
a man o' the times who yearns like Kent to be "acknowledged." Left

alone with the Duchess' body he recoils from his own depravity and decides to redeem his life by dedicating it to Antonio. (Although he lectured to his Duchess on the vanity of life, it was she who taught him "how to die.") Despite his new-found moral courage, however, Bosola never escapes from the mist of error that enshrouds his life. The Cardinal's Machiavellian tenacity temporarily blunts his moral purpose and causes him to stab Antonio, whom he would have saved. He dies still gnawed by "neglect," happy only that he has fallen "in so good a quarrell."

For Antonio there is not even this satisfaction. His contemptible death is appropriate for one who felt trapped by circumstances at the moment of his greatest happiness. When he jests with the Duchess about the deceptive joys of marriage, his lines ring pathetically true. Too knowledgeable and wary, he lacks the sublimely illusory confidence that love brings to his wife. Overwhelmed by Ferdinand's fury, he tries repeatedly to shape some safety for himself and thus he is, in spite of his soldierly abilities, ineffectual in every crisis. "Lost in amazement," he confides his fears to Delio; and though he speaks bravely of confronting Ferdinand he ignores his opportunity. When at Loretto the Duchess suggests that they part, he replies, "You councell safely"; even then he speaks of himself as spiritually dead.

When he is infinitely weary of his "pore lingering life" and despairs of saving himself by halves, he seeks a "pardon" from the Cardinal. His hope for mercy is suicidal, but he seems to know this; indeed, he is more than half in love with easeful death. He has opened inward on himself the doors of death which have such "strange geometrical hinges"; and when Bosola completes the agonizing mortification by degrees Antonio plays his own tragic chorus:

> In all our Quest of Greatnes . . .
> (Like wanton Boyes, whose pastime is their care)
> We follow after bubbles, blowne in th'ayre.
> Pleasure of life, what is't? onely the good houres
> Of an Ague: meerely a preparative to rest,
> To endure vexation.   (v. iv. 75-80)

Here is Flamineo's testament of futility softened by pathos and regret. The pity of Antonio's fate is not that he could have saved the woman he loved, but that he knew too well the hopelessness of his situation. Content to stave off disaster as long as he can, he protects his secret marriage by lies and deceptions. He grows rich "the left hand way" while rumors spread that his wife is a whore. He takes shameful ways to avoid shame because he cannot accept with dignity the fatal consequences which he so clearly foresaw.

In Bosola and Antonio, Webster cuts across conventional distinctions to illuminate the anguish of men whose lack of illusion is the greatest illusion of all. Perplexing as these characters seem to modern readers, they were no doubt recognizable to Webster's audience, who saw at court many men similarly fascinated with their dooms, fluttering like moths around the candle of advancement and hoping even in the Tower for a return to favor or a royal reconciliation, until the executioner's axe brought an end to uncertainty.

In Brachiano and Flamineo, Webster admired heroic villains who to themselves were "enough"; he sought the meaning of life in the Troll morality. We cannot judge Bosola, however, by the standard of the Gyntian self, for his mind is so divided that he is never truer to himself than when he vacillates between cynicism and compassion for the Duchess. If, as we are told, Webster celebrates the religion of self in the *Duchess*,[4] then his high priest is Ferdinand, who like the lunatics in *Peer Gynt* achieves the total absorption in self possible only to the insane. Even before his mind gives way Ferdinand lives in a continual fever of egoism that is alleviated by the complete subjugation of Bosola and his sister. We do not have to exaggerate the faint suggestions of incestuous desire to motivate Ferdinand's fury at the Duchess; even more terrible than any hints of unnatural lust is his frenzied conception of "Honor," his pitiless identification with his sister. To him her greatest sin lay in her blood, the same blood that runs through his aristocratic veins.

The Cardinal is a complementary portrait of the buried life: his diseased ego is satisfied not by a brute assertion of will but by a rational mastery of Machiavellian arts. He pursues, it would seem, the ultimate intellectual refinement of Machiavellian technique that becomes an end in itself. He does not have the Elizabethan Machiavel's instinctive appetite for horrendous crime. He has a connoisseur's taste for flawless villainy, for security in evil. On the surface he is nerveless, emotionless, so much the master of himself that even Bosola must admire his seeming fearlessness. But what appears at first to be a mastery of passion is finally revealed to be a deficiency of normal feeling, an emotional lifelessness. Delio has heard that the Cardinal is

> a brave fellow,
> Will play his five thousand crownes, at Tennis, Daunce,
> Court Ladies, and one that hath fought single Combats.

(I. i. 154-56)

Antonio knows better: "Some such flashes superficially hang on him, for forme: but observe his inward Character: he is a mellancholly

---

[4] See Nicoll's discussion of Tourneur's imitations in his "Introduction," *Works of Tourneur*, pp. 6 ff.

Churchman" (I. i. 157-58). Apart from these superficial flashes the Cardinal has no commitment to life. He spends his last hours troubled by a dull headache of remorse and bored by the whisper of his conscience. Together with Ferdinand he represents the collaboration of sadistic fury and intellectuality that lies behind the totalitarian savagery in *Lear* and in the world around us. If there is a heavy-handed irony in the manner of his death, his sudden display of cowardice is not surprising in one so expert at murdering defenseless women. Although he seemed fearless, the prospect of death unnerves him. Cringing, begging to be spared, he tries to buy off Bosola, who answers:

> Now it seemes thy Greatnes was onely outward:
> For thou fall'st faster of thy selfe, then calamitie
> Can drive thee.   (v. v. 56-58)

Though mortally wounded himself, Bosola is satisfied that the Cardinal, who

> stood'st like a huge Piramid
> Begun upon a large, and ample base,
> Shalt end in a little point, a kind of nothing.   (v. v. 96-98)

If the Cardinal has any virtue it lies in the final knowledge of his insignificance—in his request to be laid aside and forgotten.

Webster's search for a nobility that rises above enslaving circumstances, unsatisfied in the glorious villains of *The White Devil,* is consummated in his portrait of a fragile, tormented young woman kneeling before her murderers. Only he among the Jacobeans dared to find a tragic heroism in a vain, willful girl, who until her dying moments is careless of her name and blind to the responsibilities which accompany prerogative. In temperament she is a heroine of Shakespearean romantic comedy, graceful, witty, wanton and innocent at the same time, who woos and wins her husband in spite of himself. She capriciously ignores the challenge of an aristocratic life, but the challenge of death— the supreme challenge in Jacobean tragedy—she accepts boldly and triumphantly. There is a beauty in her death that makes the ugliness of Ferdinand's life unbearable and that shakes the cynical nihilism which is Bosola's defense against conscience. What begins as a vicarious purge of the filthiness of Ferdinand's mind becomes in the end a conflict of inner strength between the Duchess and her torturers. Caught in the trap that Fortune set for her she ceases to be Fortune's slave. Her murderers would drag her down and open her eyes to the "realities" which they perceive; they would have her share the horror of their lives. They bring her to her knees, but it is the posture of heaven.

They surround her with assassins but it is she who gives the last command:

> Go tell my brothers, when I am laid out,
> They then may feede in quiet.   (IV. ii. 243-44)

From the lips of a woman who has gone beyond despair we learn the annihilating truth that the power to oppress and kill is an ultimate value only to those who find death "infinitely terrible."

For the Duchess no gesture of defiance is needed to obliterate the terror of death. It is against the attempt to despoil her humanity that she flings her celebrated assertion of individuality, "I am Duchesse of *Malfy* still." Perhaps we tend to exaggerate the heroic ring of this line, which could be justly interpreted as a tremor of meaningless pride. But even if it is an expression of that quality which Chapman called "noblesse," there is no justification for removing the line from its context as *the* quintessential moment of the play. The Duchess' strength is not a lonely existential awareness of self but a remembrance of love, expressed in her parting words to Cariola and in her answers to Bosola. The spirit of woman that once betrayed now sustains her, for she knows that the fragile, "illusory" joys of devotion are the deepest certainties of human existence. Webster's other heroes and heroines die obsessed with their sins and follies, projecting their individual experiences as the pattern of man's fate. The Duchess is the only one to move out of self, to turn her thoughts outward upon those she loves and upward in serene religious faith.

More than a conventional artistic "solution," the Duchess' piety seems an intuition of a realm of values obscured by the corruption of the Church (in which the Cardinal is a Prince) and by the cant that passes for religious conviction. Yet Webster does not allow us to share the Duchess' conviction of the providential nature of her torments. As in *Lear* the characters in the *Duchess* interpret their tragic experiences in various and contradictory ways. And if any one character speaks for Webster at the close, it is not Delio, the outsider, but Bosola, who was an actor "in all the maine of all":

> Oh, this gloomy world,
> In what a shadow, or deepe pit of darknesse,
> Doth (womanish, and fearefull) mankind live!
> Let worthy mindes nere stagger in distrust
> To suffer death, or shame, for what is just—
>
>   (V. v. 124-28)

It is not the courage to be greatly evil which Bosola commends, but the courage to be greatly good in a world which offers a hundred crooked subterfuges and which demands the sham, not the reality, of virtue.

The Duchess of Malfi: Styles of Ceremony

by James L. Calderwood

In his review-article, "Motives in *Malfi*" (*Essays in Criticism,* Oct., 1959), McD. Emslie presents an interesting departure from what has been, until recently, a prevailing fashion in Webster criticism—the careful examination not so much of the plays themselves but of their literary failings. For critics with this sort of aim, Webster has been a fairly easy mark. Admissions are not difficult to make: Webster's plots are replete with the most un-Aristotelian contingencies and blind alleys; his verse, happily suited to the aphorism, is only rarely able to sustain itself well beyond a couple of lines; his action is uncomfortably near to being melodramatic; his characterization is often either vague or else too neatly Theophrastian; and finally—a fault for which some of his critics have been unable to forgive him—his plays were not written by Shakespeare. Underlying much of the specific criticism of Webster is a general distaste for his philosophy, or, more accurately, for his lack of a philosophy, for his failure to supply in his plays a governing moral perspective. For example, W. A. Edwards finds ["John Webster," *Determinations,* ed. F. R. Leavis (London, 1934), p. 176] that "in Webster's tragedies there is no such internal scale [as that provided in *Hamlet*] to measure depravity." Ian Jack holds a similar view ["The Case of John Webster," *Scrutiny,* XVI (March, 1949), p. 38]: "If one reads through [both plays] noting down the *sententia* and moralizing asides, one finds oneself in possession of a definite attempt at a 'philosophy,' a moral to the tale." However, Jack finds that the tale itself is altogether too discrete from the attempted moral. He concludes (p. 43) that the plays exemplify Webster's "artistic insincerity" and that Webster himself is a "decadent in the sense that he is incapable of realizing the whole of life in the form in which it revealed itself to the Elizabethans."

The argument of Edwards and Jack, however it may apply to *The White Devil,* seems wholly untenable with respect to *The Duchess of*

"The Duchess of Malfi: *Styles of Ceremony*" by James L. Calderwood. From Essays in Criticism, XII (1962), 133-47. Copyright © 1962 by F. W. Bateson. Reprinted by permission of the publisher.

Malfi. Certainly no one, I think, denies that the later play has an abundance of depravity and is embarrassingly rich in unintegrated moral comment, or that there are excrescences of plot and inconsistencies of character. But these faults can be granted without our having to concede either that the play is a dramatic failure or that Webster is morally despicable. On the contrary, the view offered here is that the play is, among other things, a powerful and subtle articulation of a thoroughly Elizabethan theme—the relationship between individual impulse and societal norms, specifically the religious and political doctrine of Degree. And I shall suggest that Webster, far from failing to present an "internal scale to measure depravity," is entirely willing to test evil against good. His principal dramatic means to this end is his employment of ceremony and ritual for the evaluation of private action. My intention here is to examine several crucial scenes in order to suggest how Webster's use of ceremony helps clarify some of the rather vexing problems of action, motivation, and character.

In a play which focuses so largely upon revenge and violence, motivation is unusually important. In the corruption scene of Act I Ferdinand, referring to the Duchess, says to Bosola: "she's a yong widowe, / I would not have her marry againe."

> *Bos.* No, Sir?
> *Ferd.* Doe not you aske the reason: but be satisfied,
>   I say I would not.

Bosola, whether satisfied or not, does not ask the reason; but critics have not been so easily put off. What Ferdinand later calls his "mayne cause"—his hope to have gained "An infinite masse of Treasure by her death" (IV. ii. 304) had she died without remarrying—has been unanimously disallowed by critics for having no dramatic confirmation elsewhere. On the other hand, most critics have acknowledged as at least plausible the case made by F. L. Lucas and supported by Clifford Leech that Ferdinand acts from incestuous jealousy. But Leech himself is not very happy with his proposal, for after all, he finds, "Ferdinand leaves us perplexed, not quite certain of the dramatist's purpose" [*John Webster* (London, 1951), p. 105]. However, the perplexity which he complains of is discredited—or at least so I am convinced—by his own findings. A certain haziness of motivation need not result from a corresponding haziness of authorial purpose but may be deliberately built into a character: it is Ferdinand who is unsure of himself, not Webster. From Ferdinand's "Doe not you aske the reason"—certainly an answer that makes us want to ask the reason—we can assume either that he does not understand the grounds of his behavior or that he prefers not to state them. But a flat refusal to discuss the matter is surely a poor means of concealing information, especially from a man who has been singled out precisely because he is an adept at ferreting facts. Ferdinand's brusqueness here suggests a lack of self-awareness, not so much an irritation at being questioned as a failure ever to have asked himself the same question.

It is in the following exchanges between the Duchess and her brothers that we should expect to find an indication of the motives underlying the demonic punishments of Act IV. There is clearly, even before the offence, a pressure behind Ferdinand's speech that is absent from his brother's. The Cardinal is willing to consider the prospect of a remarriage provided it involves "the addition, Honor"; Ferdinand categorically forbids it: "Marry? they are most luxurious, / Will wed twice." It is Ferdinand who harps upon the sensual temptations of re-marriage—"luxurious" (i.e., lecherous), "those joyes, / Those lustful pleasures," his Lamprey metaphor; and he associates sensuality with corruption and disease—"Their livers are more spotted / Then *Lebans* sheepe"—an association which he dwells upon again, most signifi-cantly, later in the play. Taking a cue from the Cardinal, however, Ferdinand does insert one important non-sensual objection to the Duchess' possible remarriage: he likens private marriage to "the irregu-lar Crab, / Which though't goes backward, thinkes that it goes right, / Because it goes its owne way." This is essentially an argument from Degree: the reliance upon private choice, especially when that choice descends upon an inferior, constitutes an infringement of the rigidly established social hierarchy and is, ultimately, an attack upon cosmo-logical order.

There is by no means sufficient evidence here to persuade us one way or another about the brothers' opposition to a possible remarriage. However, the Duchess provides us a critical perspective to the scene when she suggests that the brotherly duet has been a piece of staged ceremony: "I thinke this speech betweene you both was studied, / It came so roundly off." The sequence of mutually supported and elabo-rated arguments has seemed impressive; but the stylization to which the Duchess calls attention enables us to observe a schism between the form and the content of their objections. For in actuality the brothers have offered only the appearance of an argument, not any logical grounds for opposition, but merely opposition. What they have said is simply that they do not want the Duchess to remarry, but their motives have been left unclarified. Ferdinand's emotional antagonism—we cannot at this point give it a more precise title—has been both partly obfuscated and superficially ennobled by the ritual formality of a "studied" presentation. Since the brothers are wholly unaware that Antonio or anyone else is a potential, much less a favored, suitor, their argument from Degree is entirely irrelevant, at best hypothetical. But as we shall see, it is not irrelevant structurally: the hypothetical attack upon order becomes actual after the brothers' exit, when the Duchess reverses the courtly tradition in her wooing of Antonio. By comparing these two brief scenes, as well as others later on, we shall find that Webster, at times so cavalier in his disregard of dramatic consistency, can at other times unify apparently discrete elements of action by remarkably subtle nexuses of imagery and structure.

The Duchess conducts her courtship of Antonio as a staged ceremony which is in effect a casting off of the essential values represented in ceremony. As a depersonalised, formalized expression of belief and emotion, ceremony is necessarily in the service of supra-individual interests, and its participants make at least a gesture of indorsing those interests by voluntarily restricting the free play of private emotion to the symbolic pattern prescribed by the ceremonial role. Although ceremony and ritual are by no means prohibitive of individual expression —but merely impose a form upon the content of private experience— they are confirmations of order, of an order that exists to some extent regardless of the individual, even if the individual is a Duchess. Indeed, as Antonio's first speech in the play implies, it is precisely because the individual here is a Duchess—the political and moral exemplar who, if corrupt, causes "Death, and diseases through the whole land"—that her conduct has serious and even tragic implications. For what the Duchess is engaging in here is not properly ceremony but ceremony-in-reverse, a form of deceremonialization by which she divests herself of the responsibilities of her social role.

The Duchess' defection from Degree is not simply the product of impetuosity; after her brothers' exit her determination to assert herself is couched in convincing terms: "if all my royall kindred / Lay in my way unto this marriage: / I'll'd make them my low foote-steps." Nor, as her last remark to Cariola indicates, is she unaware of the broader implications of her action:

> wish me good speed
> For I am going into a wildernesse,
> Where I shall find nor path, nor friendly clewe
> To be my guide.

This journey beyond the restrictions, but also the safeguards, of Degree into a "wildernesse" where her only guides are the dictates of private impulse cannot help reminding us of Ferdinand's warning about "the irregular Crab / Which though't goes backward, thinkes that it goes right, / Because it goes its owne way." But the Duchess' "owne way" is not a random one. The "wildernesse" into which she goes may be thoroughly disordered, but her means of getting there are quite systematic.

She first establishes Degree with almost ritual formality. As Antonio enters, at her bidding, her greeting is an expression of superiority: "I sent for you, Sit downe." This is of course ironic, and charmingly so in the light of her intentions; but it is also the initial step towards a moral infraction the gravity of which charm fails to dissipate. It is also significant, particularly in a scene which makes a symbolic point of bodily positions, that at the beginning the audience is presented with a view of Antonio seated and the Duchess standing above him, prepared to dictate her "will." She quickly forces an opportunity to use the word *husband*, and then with considerable psychological subtlety suggests her concern about "What's laid up for to-morrow," which, coming hard after the word "expence," seems to regard Antonio in his inferior role as treasurer—and so he interprets it; but then she corrects him by explaining that she meant "What's layd up yonder for me," that is, in heaven, which gently insinuates Antonio into an equality with her as fellow mortal. Further promptings by the Duchess, the most important of which are of a ceremonial nature—the transfer of the ring (463), the symbolic elevation of rank (481-2)—lead Antonio to realize "whereto [her] favors tend"; but though he is tempted by ambition, he remains uncomfortably aware of his "unworthinesse," of his prescribed station in the hierarchy of Degree. To the Duchess, for whom Degree is by this time irrelevant, his hesitance is puzzling: "Sir, be confident, / What is't distracts you?" Despite his later reminder about her brothers, it is not fear of violence that is troubling Antonio: it is made sufficiently clear that he is an excellent soldier, a man of proved courage and ability. It is also made sufficiently clear that he is an honorable man, one who would be honest, as he says, "were there nor heaven, nor hell." Indeed, his distraction here could only be felt by an honorable man, for it stems from a conflict between private desire and societal values. Part of the irony of the courtship scene is that the Duchess abandons Degree in wooing the one man who thoroughly endorses Degree: his opening lines in Act I display his admiration for the French king who sought "to reduce both State, and People / To a fix'd Order." It is in the light of Antonio's reluctance to overturn Degree that Webster, by a kind of literary counterpoint, enables us to judge the nature of the Duchess' conduct. For the ceremonial revelation of her feelings to Antonio is necessitated by the inhibitions of Degree. The "great," she says,

> Are forc'd to expresse our violent passions
> In ridles, and in dreames, and leave the path
> Of simple vertue, which was never made
> To seeme the thing it is not.

It is surely a perversion of terminology when the "path of simple vertue"—which echoes her earlier image of the pathless "wildernesse"

—has become representative of uninhibited passion. Having discarded
her own loyalties to "fix'd Order," she has nevertheless been utilizing
until now the symbolic forms of order—ceremony and ritual—as psychological weapons designed to overcome Antonio's more entrenched
loyalties and to release the passions which those loyalties have so far
successfully constrained. Her final resort is to dispense altogether with
ceremony and Degree; if he will not rise to her station, she will descend
to his: "I do here put off all vaine ceremony, / And onely doe appeare
to you a yong widow / That claimes you for her husband." It is a telling expedient, and with it Antonio's last resistance breaks. It is characteristic of him that he is unable either to deceive effectively—witness
the way he falls apart in ii. iii, when forced into deceptions—or to
cope with deception. But it must be admitted that the Duchess' tech-
niques—first establishing, then suddenly relaxing the formalities of
Degree—have been unusually subtle, and, coupled with his own desires, difficult to resist.

Near the conclusion of this movement away from Degree and towards the release of "violent passions," we have another brief ritual
gesture as the Duchess puts her arms around Antonio and then orders
him to kneel. It is a fitting end, for the gesture is merely a gesture;
far from endorsing ceremony and the values it represents, the Duchess
engages in a profane parody, employing the ritual solemnities of Degree to confirm and sanction the autonomy of private impulse, the
symbols of order to proclaim the ascendancy of disorder. Of her brothers she says:

> Do not thinke of them,
> All discord, without this circumference
> Is onely to be pittied, and not feared:
> Yet, should they know it, time will easily
> Scatter the tempest.

The imagery here, and in the following passages which use musical
metaphors (551-4), is strongly reminiscent of Ulysses' famous speech
on Degree in *Troilus and Cressida*: "Take but degree away, untune
that string, / And, hark, what discord follows" (i. iii. 109-10 ff.).[1]
Degree taken away, discord does indeed follow; but for the moment the

---

[1] In some respects Webster's entire play is a comment on Shakespeare's passage,
even to the point of Ferdinand's becoming, like "appetite," a "universal wolf" eat-
ing himself up in madness. Incidentally, there is another parallel with Shakespeare
that has gone unmentioned: in iv. ii, Bosola, denied reward for his services to
Ferdinand, says, "I stand like one / That long hath ta'ne a sweet, and golden
dreame. / I am angry with my selfe, now that I wake" (349-50), which appears to
be an echo of Posthumous' speech in *Cymbeline* (v. iv. 127-9), "And so I am
awake. Poor wretches, that depend / On greatness' favour, dream as I have done, /
Wake, and find nothing."

lovers seek within the circumference of their own arms to create a private universe, to elevate "violent passion" to the status of a self-sufficient moral law. The attempt may have its romantic appeal, but the Duchess' speech displays a disrespect for external realities which is, as the remainder of the play demonstrates, dangerously naïve. It is left to Cariola to conclude the scene on a note of ominousness: "Whether the spirit of greatnes, or of woman / Raigne most in her, I know not, but it shewes / A fearefull madnes. I owe her much of pitty."

If we are correct in assuming that Webster is using ceremony as a dramatic device to explore subtleties of character and action, we should expect it to be used again in other critical scenes. The tragic ironies of the Duchess' speech about "discord" indicate that Webster was anticipating the dramatic future. The audience is prepared for the next appearance of Ferdinand and the Cardinal, is awaiting with a certain amount of suspense the brothers' reactions to the marriage. In ii. iv, where those reactions are presented, Webster is clearly conscious of the logical and structural claims imposed upon him by Act I. The "tempest" which the Duchess felt time would scatter has now arisen in the form of Ferdinand's intemperate anger; the association is made exact as the Cardinal says, "Why doe you make your selfe / So wild a Tempest?" and Ferdinand wishes the metaphor were literal fact: "Would I could be one. . . ." Ferdinand also embodies the "discord" of which the Duchess was so disdainful: he produces "this intemperate noyce," and is admonished by the Cardinal, "Come, put your selfe / In tune." His anger, we may think, is perhaps a vastly amplified echo of Antonio's "distraction"—that is, that just as Antonio hesitated to over-turn Degree, so Ferdinand rages because it has been overturned. But this would hardly explain the Cardinal's relative calmness, his utter inability to comprehend his brother's reactions: "You flie beyond your reason"; "Are you starke mad?" Only if we accept the unmistakable suggestions of incestuous jealousy in this scene does Ferdinand's be-havior become more understandable for us than for the Cardinal.

The psychological development here is roughly the reverse of that in Act I. Instead of casting off ceremony to reveal underlying passions, Ferdinand moves from passion to the cloaking of passion in ceremonial robes, from disorder to order. His opening line, "I have this night dig'd up a man-drake," is meaningfully ambiguous, carrying not only the primary notion of madness but a secondary, sexual implication as well. What is merely implication at this point becomes manifest when Ferdinand's sense of injury shifts to the source of injury:

> Me thinkes I see her laughing,
> Excellent *Hyenna*—talke to me somewhat, quickly,
> Or my imagination will carry me
> To see her, in the shamefull act of sinne.

To this point, and somewhat beyond it, Ferdinand seems wholly lack-
ing in self-awareness; his jealousy receives direct expression in anger,
but he is conscious only of anger, and mistakenly assumes that the
Cardinal is reacting similarly. But when he tortures himself with images of the Duchess "in the shamefull act" (56-9) he has clearly gone
beyond anything that the Cardinal is feeling. The intensity of his experience is attested by his failure even to hear the Cardinal's "You flie
beyond your reason." Lost to the immediate situation, he directly
addresses his sister from his imaginative station as voyeur (62-4).
Dumbfounded by this display, the Cardinal remonstrates with a metaphor that is more accurate than he realizes:

> this intemperate noyce,
> Fitly resembles deafe-mens shrill discourse,
> Who talke aloud, thinking all other men
> To have their imperfection.

Although Ferdinand is unconscious of the nature of his "imperfec-
tion," he has supposed a similar violence of reaction on the part of
his brother. It is only now that he senses a difference between them.
Immediately he withdraws, knowing that he has somehow exposed
himself. His next lines—"Have not you, / My palsy?"—mark an abrupt
shift of tone: outwardly directed anger recoils, turns inward, gives way
to self-suspicion. The question is wary, the diction ambiguous enough
to suggest shaking anger and perhaps also his half-awareness of a
deeper motivation springing from bodily disturbance. The Cardinal's
reply is significant:

> Yes—I can be angry
> Without this rupture—there is not in nature
> A thing, that makes man so deform'd, so beastly,
> As doth intemperate anger . . .

The thought moves from the personal to the general, from the admission of private but controlled anger to an explanation of the necessity
of control. Disordered passions, whether specifically sexual or not,
represent a deviation from the nature of, from what is proper to, man;
it is not Ferdinand's impulse to violence that the Cardinal objects to,
it is the unrestrained disorder of that impulse. The parallel with the
Duchess is obvious: both have become threats to society by departing
from communal patterns of ordered behavior, by representing the
chaos of uninhibited private action. But the parallel ends there. Ferdinand has not deliberately violated Degree in order to release passion; indeed, his very lack of deliberation, the spontaneity of his giving way to emotion, has released to the surface a deformity of man's
nature. Although both of them enter a "wildernesse," the Duchess

seeks to establish private order amid public disorder, to forge a circumference of harmony in the center of discord. Secure of self, conscious of her own identity, she conceives of "wildernesse" as being purely external. But Ferdinand blunders into a chaos within himself. Nearly losing complete control of himself, he discovers a self he would prefer to lose. Ultimately he does lose himself all ways, in madness; and ultimately the Duchess retains her self, even triumphantly reasserts her identity despite all Ferdinand can do to destroy her.

Webster's problem now is a delicate one. Unless the prolonged torture and demonic killing of the Duchess have some amount of communal sanction, he will have produced, not tragedy, but only melodrama. Having already suggested the potential tragic justification by presenting the Duchess' marriage as a violation of Degree, he now runs the risk of causing Ferdinand to exact disproportionate retribution as a private agent; the nexus between crime and punishment is in danger of breaking. Webster's solution is to cement that nexus by an inversion of the process which led to the crime.

Throughout II. iv, Ferdinand employs the imagery which will lead him from private to at least a semblance of public revenge. From the beginning his mind dwells upon purgation:

> We must not now use Balsamum, but fire,
> The smarting cupping-glasse, for that's the meane
> To purge infected blood, (such blood as hers:).

If the sin is of the blood, as Vittoria's was in *The White Devil,* the blood must pay for it. But this medical imagery, which suggests an impulse towards impersonal action—Ferdinand as agent of society, the physician-priest who will restore order by destroying disorder—is unconvincing in light of the private animus manifest in Ferdinand's outbursts. But there is, as we noted, a shift of tone following the Cardinal's remonstrance about "deafe-mens shrill discourse," a shift of tone which mirrors Ferdinand's shift in self-consciousness. After the Cardinal's next speech, which concludes with an exhortation to order— "Come, put your selfe / In tune"—Ferdinand, already sobered by self-doubt, returns a premeditated answer:

> So—I will onely study to seeme
> The thing I am not . . .

To pause briefly here, we should note the verbal echo from Act I where the Duchess, lamenting the inhibitions imposed by greatness, spoke of "simple vertue, which was never made / To seeme the thing it is not" (513-14), just before she "put off all vaine ceremony." Here, however, Ferdinand intends just the reverse—to submit passion to order, or at least to the appearance of order. He continues:

> . . . I could kill her now,
> In you, or in my selfe, for I do thinke
> It is some sinne in us, Heaven doth revenge
> By her.

This is an entirely new turn of thought, to which the Cardinal can only react with amazement: "Are you starke mad?" But this is a far cry from madness. If we have been correct in gauging his growth of self-awareness, Ferdinand's acknowledgement of "some sinne in us" which requires expiation employs the plural "us" merely as a cover: the sin is within him alone, and he knows it. More significant, however, is his identification of his with the Duchess' sin, the linking of his latent desire with her realized desire; for here is precisely the association needed to justify his revenge upon her and to expiate his own latent sin: he can now truly quench his "wild-fire" with her "whores blood." What would have been merely a private act of violence now assumes the status of ritual purgation, with the Duchess as sacrificial scapegoat and Ferdinand, already her judge, as physician-priest-executioner who seeks the purgation of his own tainted blood in the purging of hers. Before the scene closes, Ferdinand reverts to the language of violence once more, but it is clear that he has found his solution. His final speech reveals an attitude far more terrifying than his earlier bluster, for it portends not merely an uninhibited, formless act of revenge but a patient, controlled, impersonal ceremony which will culminate with the Duchess' execution.

All of this is not of course to suggest that the highly ceremonialized murder of IV. ii, is justified merely because it is ceremonial, nor that Ferdinand is genuinely identified with moral order merely because he converts an essentially private vengeance into the appearance of public justice. Ferdinand's role is obviously synthetic, an attempt to dignify incestuous frustrations that urge him to retaliation. Yet by restraining his desire for immediate vengeance, and, more important, by transforming it and his sexual desires as well into elements of a formal process, he makes a gesture of sublimation which, even though synthetic, suggests a confirmation of order. It is a gesture entirely appropriate to the nature of the Duchess' marriage, for if the crime is against society, the punishment must in some sense proceed from society. It is owing to this ritualization of vengeance that we apprehend the inevitability of disaster so important in tragedy, an inevitability which arises only from our consciousness of extra-personal forces working out the fate of the protagonist.[2]

---

[2] For the relationship between private action and communal order, I am indebted to Professor Robert B. Heilman's excellent book on *Othello—Magic in the Web* (Lexington, Kentucky, 1956)—and especially to his chapter, "Othello: Action and Language," pp. 137-168.

In IV. i, the ritual begins. The Duchess has been imprisoned for an indeterminate period. Ferdinand consults Bosola about her behavior, seems satisfied to learn of her nobility. But when Bosola remarks that her blood is not altogether subdued, indeed that her very imprisonment away from Antonio "Makes her too passionately apprehend / Those pleasures she's kept from," Ferdinand responds with his own brand of passion:

> Curse upon her!
> I will no longer study in the booke
> Of anothers heart: informe her what I told you.

The nature of his feelings and the difficulty with which he keeps them subjected to the demands of ceremony are always most apparent when some sensual reference to the Duchess' "whores blood" reignites his "wild-fire." But he always manages to regain control, to depersonalize the issue. When Bosola remonstrates with him (142-6) and unfortunately mentions the Duchess' "delicate skinne," Ferdinand's reply again reveals a momentary breakdown of his role: "Damne her, that body of hers. . . ." He resolves upon further torments: so long as the sacrificial victim lives, so long as the Duchess' blood remains unregenerate, the latent sin within himself continues unpurged. More drastic purgatives having been planned, he resumes his role: "Intemperate agues, make Physitians cruell" (170).

In IV. ii, a new development occurs. The increasing imbalance of Ferdinand's mind is suggested by his changing to a form of homeopathic treatment in which the mad are to heal the mad. He is still attempting to purge himself by proxy, but his employment of madmen symbolizes his own approaching madness. His identification of his own sin with that of the Duchess has led him to impute to her, not just sensuality, but all of his aberrations. The strain of holding in balance the conflicting demands of the synthetic role and private passion, the inevitable self-injury involved in destroying the object of desire, and the impossibility of genuinely purging himself by means of another— all are contributing to Ferdinand's mental disintegration. As the Duchess grows more confirmed in her personal identity (139), he begins to lose all sense of identity in that "wildernesse" within him.

The conclusion of the ritual is the Duchess' sacrificial death. Bosola engages in his own form of depersonalization, assuming the role of bellman both to conceal and to dignify his participation in what he has come to regard as an extravagant cruelty. Ironically enough, the ceremony designed to purify Ferdinand has served to purify Bosola, for by experiencing the Duchess' integrity of self it is he who has metamorphosed from an impersonal agent of Ferdinand's malice to a re-

sponsible individual capable of the independent action he performs in
the last act of the play.

In the dialogue with Bosola over the Duchess' body, Ferdinand, rapidly nearing madness, achieves what appears to be a form of *anagnori-*
sis. He acknowledges both the fact and the injustice of the private act
of vengeance: "I bad thee, when I was distracted of my wits, / Goe kill
my dearest friend, and thou hast don't" (298-9). But the admission of
injustice is in the abstract, and, qualified by the emphasis upon Bosola
as efficient cause and by the claim of mental distraction, it is in effect
merely a denial of personal responsibility. Appeals to justification on
the grounds of ritual authority—Ferdinand as physician-priest serving
society—are conspicuously absent. For evaluation from that point of
view, however, we have only to wait a few lines, until Ferdinand says:

> By what authority did'st thou execute
> This bloody sentence?
> *Bos.* By yours—
> *Ferd.* Mine? was I her Judge?
> Did any ceremoniall forme of Law,
> Doombe her to not-Being?

The denial of "any ceremoniall forme of Law," of any communally
sanctioned process by which revenge was executed, is aimed at depriv-
ing Bosola of reward, but instead deprives Ferdinand himself of that
superficial ennoblement of motive which he had sought through an
alliance with the forms of order. It is one of Ferdinand's last rational
utterances, and it is thoroughly appropriate that as he approaches the
disaster of mind which is correlative with the Duchess' death, Webster
chooses to illumine the nature of Ferdinand's revenge by the same
dramatic technique with which he illumined the nature of her offence:
it is Webster's final use of ceremony as an "internal scale to measure
depravity."

Distancing in *The Duchess of Malfi*

by Clifford Leech

The deliberateness of *The Duchess of Malfi* is brought home to us, too, in the different modes of distancing that Webster uses. And of course we must recognize that such distancing is necessary for two reasons. The Greek dramatists had a chorus, which both generalized from the particular instance of the play's action and, by referring to the past that lay behind the play's events or by invoking a setting and an atmosphere remote from the immediate issue, sketched a total image of the world which was the context of the play's being. The Elizabethans and Jacobeans had no such ready device, but they could switch the attention by an interjaculated scene or by a speech that looked back or forward, or in its manner was remote from everyday usage, so that the play's individual story was not merely (though it was also) a special case. In *Antony and Cleopatra* we may think of the scene on Pompey's galley, where the three masters of the world in their cups are, without knowing it, at the mercy of Pompey's reluctant honor, or of the scene in Asia Minor where Ventidius dare not do too well on Antony's behalf lest the victory of a subordinate should gall the general, or of Enobarbus's speech on Cleopatra, which both looks to the past and justifies the present. At such moments we are not immediately involved with the passing event: we have the leisure to consider, we see the framework of space and time within which the event takes place. The interventions of the story-teller in Brecht's *The Caucasian Chalk Circle* operate in much the same way. Webster had particular need, however, for some devices of this sort. In this play and in *The White Devil* he had stories of peculiar intimacy and dreadfulness to tell. He wanted to assert the general truth of the action— that is, he wanted to suggest that his tragic conflict and its consequences were emblems of things known to man as part of his condition —and he wanted to interpose moments of relaxation to avoid the numbing effect of a persistent pageant of woe. We know well enough

"Distancing in The Duchess of Malfi*" (Editor's title) by Clifford Leech. From* Webster: The Duchess of Malfi *(London: Edward Arnold, Publishers, Ltd., 1963), pp. 35-40. Copyright © 1963 by Clifford Leech. Reprinted by permission of the publisher.*

in actuality that, when misfortunes come in full battalions, their edge is blunted. The high points of misfortune in tragedy may effectively take an audience unaware but not when they are unready. So-called "comic relief" is of limited use for this purpose, though, if the absurdity is in tune with the tragic event, if it has the right acrid quality, it will in some measure do. Webster uses it in Bosola's railing at the Old Lady and Castruchio in Act II. But this in plenty will defeat itself, becoming expected and blunted, and it may overwhelm the tragic event in frivolity. So other devices had to be found. Webster's solutions to the problem were not all equally successful, but at least we should recognize their purpose.

The first method we may notice is the use of interposed fables, which Rupert Brooke called "long-winded, irrelevant, and fantastically unrealistic tales." [1] Webster had used the device in *The White Devil*—in II. i, where Francisco tells Camillo a story of Apollo's projected wedding and the general protest caused by the fear that the sun might beget many suns, and in IV. ii, where Flamineo tells Bracciano and Vittoria the tale of the ungrateful crocodile and the bird that flies into its mouth to relieve it of pain. In both these instances the fable is a roundabout way to persuade without over-blunt speaking: Camillo is to see to it that his wife Vittoria does not become pregant; Bracciano is to remember with gratitude the services Flamineo has done him. The indirectness of the communication is underlined when, in the later instance, Flamineo produces an alternative explanation. But the device is used not merely for tact. The extended narration, the turning to another story (however much of an allegory it is), take us away from the immediate presence of lust and murder and revenge. In *The Duchess of Malfi* we also have two instances of the device, more surprisingly but more tellingly used. We have seen that the meeting of Ferdinand and the Duchess in her bed chamber in III. ii. is the play's central point, the moment of reversal in that thereafter the brother and sister change places, and the end of the slow climb to discovery and the beginning of the plunge to disaster. As Ferdinand is about to leave her, he breaks off his imprecations to tell her of how Reputation, Love and Death came to journey through the world and planned to take separate paths—Death to battlefields and plague-stricken cities, Love to the dwellings of "unambitious shepherds" and penniless orphans—but Reputation urged the others not to leave him, for, once he had parted company with a man, he was never to be found again. It is a twelve-line intermission from the direct encounter of the two characters: the audience is invited to think in general terms, in allegorical abstracts, on a subject that is only tangential to the Duchess's

[1] *John Webster and the Elizabethan Drama,* 1916, p. 130.

story. Yet, though tangential, it is relevant enough: the Duchess has
defied Reputation, the world's good word, the world's and the word's
power over her. Listening, we lean away from the joined conflict, but
are not allowed to forget it. Then suddenly we are plunged back, with
Ferdinand's departure and the disturbed reappearance of Antonio and
Cariola. The second instance of the device comes almost at the end of
Act III, when the Duchess has been arrested by Bosola and his guards.
She breaks from straightforward protest to tell the story of a salmon
and a dog-fish. The rough fish of the sea rebukes the salmon for leaving its river and venturing to the sea without showing a proper respect
for its native-born citizens. The salmon replies that their respective
worths will not be known till they are both netted and sold for cook-
ing. It is an allegorical challenge to the world's great, appropriate because in the following act the Duchess is to die and Bosola and his
master will then be led to death. In the immediate context it is in de-
fence of Antonio that the Duchess speaks, but her words have more
powerful, if grotesque, relevance to her own position. And, after the
sadness of her parting from her husband, we are given this opportunity to stand back from the present before entering on the ceremony
of woe that will occupy Act IV.

There is no doubt that these interposed fables in Webster's tragedies
constitute an oddity for most modern readers. We can hardly guess
how they sounded in 1612-14. Yet we can see why they were used, and
in attentive reading (less certainly in performance) they can have their
proper effect today.

The next device of this kind to be mentioned is also foreign to a
modern audience. This is the use of the "sentence" or *sententia,* commonly reinforced by rhyme. Thus in i. i, Antonio compares a prince's
court to a fountain from which "Pure silver drops" should flow, and
he then gives the warning:

> but if't chance
> Some curs'd example poison 't near the head,
> *Death, and diseases through the whole land spread.*[2]

(I. i. 13-15)

A modern audience is not used to rhyme, but will accept it when employed facetiously or in a fantastic situation (in *A Midsummer Night's
Dream,* for example): today rhyme will seem inappropriate in an utterance deliberately embodying wisdom or showing strong feeling. This is
partly because, of our older dramatists, Shakespeare alone dominates

---

[2] In the original Quarto a sentence-line is commonly preceded by quotation marks
and, in addition, is sometimes printed in italics. In J. R. Brown's Revels edition,
italics are uniformly used for the purpose.

the modern stage. He used rhyme frequently in his earlier plays but moved from it later. So Webster's rhymes here will jar, seeming at odds with the temper of the utterance. In fact, Webster probably uses rhyme less frequently than Chapman, whose tragedies were written in almost the same years as Shakespeare's: the Jacobeans had not read that rhyme was a sign of early dating. Moreover, the sentence is generally less directly employed in the mature Shakespeare. It can be a facetious utterance, as with Iago in *Othello,* ii. i, where he improvises verses on the natures of women, or it is given a personal impress and an impress appropriate to the situation. Macbeth, contemplating the nature of life in v. v, speaks in terms fitting himself and his situation when his wife is dead and power is slipping away. Chapman and Webster, on the other hand, use the generalized utterance in an impersonal, unparticularized form. There is nothing to tell us, save the speech-heading, who the speaker is. That does not make it poor drama: if a playwright wishes, he can depersonalize a character as Shakespeare did with Casca in *Julius Caesar,* i. iii. Unlike Shakespeare, Webster will use such a depersonalized speaker for a direct choric utterance. And he will use the sentence, with its clanging rhyme, even at a point of emotional intensity, as with the Duchess immediately she has cursed the stars and her brothers:

> Let them, like tyrants,
> Never be remember'd but for the ill they have done;
> Let all the zealous prayers of mortified
> Churchmen forget them!—
> *Bos.*   O, uncharitable!
> *Duch.* Let heaven, a little while, cease crowning martyrs,
> To punish them!
> Go howl them this: and say I long to bleed:
> *It is some mercy, when men kill with speed.*   (iv. i. 103-10)

The employment of this device grows more frequent, indeed, in *The Duchess of Malfi* and *The White Devil* as they move towards a peak. Just as Webster's use of locality was a varying one, shifting between constriction, contrast and dispersal, so in his use of dialogue he moved from the strongly personal and particularized to the generalized. The sentences are short, a single line or a couplet, but there are enough of them to give the impression of a tendency to change the dramatic focus. If a modern audience finds the varying technique a distraction, it should be reminded of the alternation of dialogue and chorus in Greek tragedy.

We have already noted the distancing-effect in the use of theater-images at iv. ii. 8, iv. ii. 36, iv. ii. 288-90, v. v. 95-6, and in the echo-device of v. iii. But perhaps the strongest example of this kind of effect is to be found dispersed through Act V, coming into most direct expression through the echo-scene but inherent in the whole last movement of the play. It is a commonplace of Webster criticism that *The Duchess of Malfi* falls into anticlimax in Act V, with the Duchess dead and only a huddle of murders to follow. There is some truth in the criticism, for the presentation of Ferdinand's grotesque raving, Bosola's uneasy and fumbling pursuit of virtue, the Cardinal's sudden maladroitness, is more impressive as a scheme than as part of an acted play. But the intention is surely to suggest the presence of the dead Duchess haunting those who have lived along with her. She is mentioned in every scene; her murder is the immediate cause of every detail of the action here; Ferdinand dies invoking her. Webster does not need her ghost—he is content to make a dubious echo speak for her, borrowing Antonio's words—but her presence is meant to be felt as that of the dead Julius Caesar in the concluding scenes of Shakespeare's play. And the effect of this is to reduce the stature of those still alive in the fifth act: they are haunted men who cannot escape the disembodied judgment that hangs in the air. So, in their loss of stature, in the now patent impotence of the individual will, they become almost the "maggots" that Rupert Brooke believed to be the only inhabitants of a Webster play.[3] That was a short-sighted view of the two major tragedies when seen as wholes, but it will do, approximately, for the last act of *The Duchess*. These men acting out their doom are, to change the image, seen through the wrong end of the telescope. We may at moments find the horrible and the pitiful in what happens to them, but we are not properly involved in the immediate event. We ceased to feel such an involvement at the end of Act IV, and we cannot much doubt that this effect was deliberate.

[3] *Op. cit.,* p. 158.

Mine Eyes Dazzle

by William Empson

This handbook by Professor Clifford Leech on *The Duchess of Malfi* is scholarly and up-to-date, and also betrays a certain delicacy of feeling. As he is strictly bound by our ridiculous fashion, he has to argue that the author and the first audiences were jeering at the Duchess for her carnal lust, and the book gives the horrid little "proofs" of it, but one feels that he dislikes the duty and mitigates it so far as he can.

Since this view of the Duchess cannot be presented on the stage, because an audience rejects it, the academic critics can give no help to the dramatic producers, so the dramatic critics, when the play is revived, usually praise the production for guying the sensationalism of the Elizabethans. There is a bit of tradition behind this idea, so that it gives a useful hint; the trouble about having learned the neo-Christian tradition, on the other hand, is that it cuts you off from any real tradition. Webster may sensibly be regarded as a precursor of Monk Lewis and Mrs. Radcliffe, and what they were being "sensational" about was the wickedness of Roman Catholic southern Europeans. Neo-Christian critics have to pretend that everybody has always been an Anglo-Catholic, so they have no idea of what the play meant to its first audiences.

We are commonly told that Webster and Tourneur, with their characters like "coiling asps" (Mermaid edition), were describing the harm often done by loss of religious faith to the Londoners around them. But an Elizabethan would say of *The White Devil* what a Victorian did of *Antony and Cleopatra*, "How unlike the domestic life of *our* beloved Queen!" The English felt culturally and socially inferior beside Italians and Spaniards, and felt it a duty to try to catch up; but also took comfort in remembering that we were good and they were very wicked, partly because they had such a wicked religion. Webster would be astonished to have his Italians taken for Englishmen. Not long ago Student Drama Society at Sheffield put on *The Revenger's*

"Mine Eyes Dazzle" by William Empson. From Essays in Criticism, *XIV (1964), 80-86. Copyright © 1964 by F. W. Bateson. Reprinted by permission of the publisher.*

Tragedy, and I was reflecting how innocent the young people seemed, as they threw themselves into their parts with all the pleasure of fancy, when I realized with a jolt that this was what Tourneur had done too. His aristocratic villains felt to him very remote, indeed I suspect they are often just unlifelike.

I realize that Belleforest and Painter, the French and English pedants who report the story, scold the Duchess for marrying her butler (unlike the Italian source); Mr. F. L. Lucas showed a firm grasp of tradition by remarking that this was ungentlemanly of them. The theater usually backs the young lovers against the Arranged Marriage, and the Globe Theatre, having a mass audience, was ready to rebuke the pride of lineage of Arragon. Thus the Duchess is a heroine; Painter or Clifford Leech would have been hooted in that theater if they had voiced their sentiments about her. One character in a play for the Globe, indeed, does talk about a romantic marriage as we are now told that everybody in the audience would have talked; it is Iago, and the playwright does not assume that the audience will agree with him. However, as Miss Bradbrook said long ago, the play is also in part a Discussion Drama, like those of Bernard Shaw, questioning whether the Duchess ought to have married the butler. I know this sounds very Philistine, after the great anti-intellectual movement, but any good theater discusses matters of current interest. Still, a play can give the pleasure of debate without leaving any doubt which side the author is on. The moral of this play, driven home as with the sledge-hammer of Dickens I should have thought, is not that the Duchess was wanton but that her brothers were sinfully proud.

My opponents argue that the Duchess and her husband make a number of anticlerical or free-thinking remarks, which would turn the audience against them; and though she becomes pious just before her death, accepting her punishment, this only gives a further indication that we are meant to think of it as partly deserved. Rather an interesting bit of historical background is needed here. Aquinas lays down (Sum. Theo.; Q. 42.1., Q. 45.5., Q. 63.2.) that marriage, even the second marriage of a woman, is a sacrament, and its sufficient cause is consent "expressed in words of the present" (that is, not a betrothal); the priest's blessing does not validate a marriage, and indeed is not given at the second marriage of a woman. However, not to solemnize a marriage is a sin. A footnote to the translation by the English Dominicans explains that Aquinas was giving the Canon Law of his time, but that clandestine marriages were declared invalid by the Council of Trent. This Council, during the middle years of the sixteenth century, tightened up a number of points of discipline by way of inaugurating the Counter-Reformation, and was of course not accepted by Protestants. The events of the play had taken place before

the change in the law, but probably most of the audience would be
vague about these dates. When her brother tells her that her children
are bastards, and she answers:

> You violate a sacrament of the Church
> Shall make you howl in Hell for it

she is in the right, considering her date; but anyhow a legal Discussion is going on, and only the horrible flabby aestheticism of our
present fashion would refuse to recognize it. A fanatical Protestant, I
suppose, would say that the new law arrogated power to priests and
encouraged breach of promise in seducers, but the Church of England
was rather inclined to favor it; a play which treated the question as
open was not likely to frighten the licensing authority. The Duchess
and her husband are presented as reasonable and practical—"Our sort
of people," as Professor Leech rightly puts it (though the Duchess is
aristocratic in her exceptional courage), so the audience would think
of them as souls naturally Protestant. All the phrases which have
been found irreligious, and therefore likely to make the audience con-
demn the Duchess and her husband (for example, the assumption
that pilgrimages deserve no reverence), are simply Protestant. Antonio, though a cautious speaker, also contrives a reference to one of
the major disputed points of doctrine. Asked what he thinks of marriage, he says:

> I take it, as those that deny Purgatory;
> It locally contains or Hell or Heaven.

This crack of course is meant to make him seem charming, as well as
sturdily sensible and right-thinking; the idea that the Globe audience
would expect him to be punished for his flippancy is very overstrained.

Modern critics usually call him cowardly, because he is so aware of
his wife's danger, just as they call her irresponsible for her courage.
But it was standard bourgeois opinion that a second husband should
not be dashing or flashy; with a sober businesslike man, the theoretical
objections would not be raised. Thus, in a way, his character is sacri-
ficed to make the audience accept the Duchess. To allow the separation
when she goes to her brothers alone was fatal in the result, but Ferdinand loves her and has demanded to have Antonio kept out of his
sight, so the plan is worth trying as a last chance; when it goes wrong,
Antonio follows her with courage ("very near my home"). In the second scene of the play we are told he has won the ring at jousting, to
prove that he is a gentleman in all but his origins. A play intended as
a warning against marrying a social inferior would have to be constructed quite differently.

Professor Clifford Leech has an argument of his own to prove that the Duchess is an irresponsible ruler; as usual, it goes bang in the opposite direction as soon as you examine the text. The Duchess is so devoted to her city state that we never hear her personal name, and she marries the man who is already administering it in the way she approves. Naturally he spends rather more as her husband. Later on she asks him what people say; he says they think she is letting him get hold of a lot of her own money, unwillingly no doubt, but on the calculation that then he won't squeeze money from the people. That is, the people know that they are unusually well governed, or at least lightly taxed, and try to invent some amusingly bad reason for it, but even in doing so confess they realize that the Duchess wishes them well. If she had married a grand husband, he would [be] pretty sure to squeeze Malfi for his private vanity or his quarrels. As the case stands, the only person who seems politically irresponsible is the Professor.

Modern critics often claim that the Duchess admits, shortly before she dies, that she was wrong to marry Antonio, or at least the Imagery there, having so much Hell about it, makes her remarks amount to that. Such critics would also claim to be defending the high old moral tradition, now all but lost; whereas any ordinary citizen could tell that they are being quaintly low-minded. A number of people in the seventeenth century actually did meet death with saintly impertinence towards the tyrant who killed them, thanking him for the gift of martyrdom, which had done them all the good in the world: "Minds innocent and quiet take That for a hermitage." If anything could have knocked them off their perch, poor creatures, it would have been to have a modern neo-Christian come up and say how pleased he was to find them licking the boots of the tyrant at the last, as it made a very edifying picture. I can't tell you how old it makes me feel, to have lived on into this eerie cultural twilight.

When the Duchess proposes marriage to her major-domo, we are usually told that he betrays ambition by accepting, but Clifford Leech is inclined to think that she tricked him into the fatal marriage; his luke-warm polite answer would not have bound him if she had not hidden a witness behind the curtain. So far from that, knowing that she is asking him to accept a post of danger, she hides the witness to make him free to refuse; in the presence of her maid, he might well feel that a refusal would make her lose too much face. We have already heard him tell a friend that he loves her, so we need not doubt it when we hear him hesitate because of the danger to her, not to himself. Both the lovers in this scene show delicacy of feeling, and the struggle of modern critics to display high-mindedness by finding something dirty in its strikes me as very queer.

We may now approach the famous Incest Problem, which arose because Freud expected audiences to be unconscious and English critics did not know what an Elizabethan audience would be conscious of. Elizabethans believed that Lucrezia Borgia went to bed with her brothers because, owing to her intense family pride, which was like that of the Pharaohs, she could find no fit mate elsewhere. The incestuous reflections of Ferdinand would thus be obvious to the first audiences, as a standard expression of the insane pride which is almost his only characteristic (at the start of the play, he forbids his courtiers to laugh unless he laughs first); no wonder he turns into a wolf in the last act, as one hoped he would. In short, the play has a popular Dickensian moral, against the wicked rich; whereas our critical attempt to recover the ethics of a nobler age has been limited to recovering subservient or boot-licking morals.

You may answer that, although many spectators would feel an easy sentiment in favor of the lovers, their serious conviction would be that the Duchess was wrong to marry her major-domo. Some would think so, no doubt; the idea that everyone held the same opinion at a given date, "the opinion of the time," is disproved as soon as you open a history book and find a lot of them killing each other because they disagreed. But there was a reason why this question was especially open to doubt, so that hardly anyone could feel the whole truth lay with Painter and Belleforest. Many subtle pages in the Variorum edition of *Twelfth Night* offer meanings for *Strachey* in "There is example for it; the lady of the Strachey married the yeoman of the wardrobe"; the answer is that Shakespeare had hunted for a meaningless word because the meaning which would be presumed was dangerous. The widow of the national hero Prince Hal, whether or not she actually married her Gentleman of the Wardrobe, in their brief and harried life together, had made him the ancestor of the entire Tudor Dynasty. It would strike the groundlings as probable that the Duchess too had made a momentous decision, and I think this explains what is usually called one of the mistakes of the play, the unhistorical choice of her surviving son by Antonio as the next Duke of Malfi. English critics tend to regard Dukedoms as ancestral, but the first husband of the Duchess had merely been given the job, presumably through the influence of her brothers. Now that they are both dead and discredited the normal influence of the town council may carry some weight, and Delio is speaking for them when he pronounces that this boy deserves the position. His horoscope would no doubt be right in predicting an early end, but I expect Webster thought of him as lasting long enough to establish a dynasty.

Perhaps I should try to make clear my assumptions about the audience. It was predominantly artisan, and the real Puritans would not come. Such an audience, like most of the population, would readily admire aristocratic courage and independence; but they would be especially prone to blame the family pride which destroys the lovers. Readily, again, they would side with their own Protestant Government against wicked Spanish grandees; but the nagging theoretical Puritanism of our present mentors would be remote from their sympathies; they would welcome the detail about keeping down the taxes.

PART TWO

View Points

Barrett Wendell

But human power has its historical stages. There are moments when, like Marlowe's and that of the lyric poets before and around him, it exerts itself in breaking old bonds; there are moments when, for a little while—as with Shakspere, and some of the lesser men at whom we have glanced—it seems free; but there must swiftly come later moments when self-consciousness begins to be inhibitory, when every effort seems to be a conscious one to struggle against the tightening force of new bonds. Webster's power always seems thus inhibited. His work is a wonderful example of how, in any school of art, a crushing sense of fact is sure fatally to overpower the surgent imagination which has lately awakened that art from lethargy to life.

So far as personal record goes, Webster's history is shadowy; and among the few plays he has left us, two will serve our purpose—the colossal sketch he called the *White Devil,* and the later, far more finished, *Duchess of Malfi.* At first sight, both seem almost crabbedly obscure; on fresh readings both reveal more and more beauties. But, no matter how well you know them, neither ever approaches the lucidity of Marlowe or of Shakspere; and this, chiefly, I think, because throughout them both every touch seems to have demanded conscious, deliberate effort. The stories of both are Italian. The former is essentially historical; Vittoria Accoramboni was alive thirty years before this dramatic account of her career was printed. The *Duchess of Malfi* comes from an older story, which found its way into Paynter's *Palace of Pleasure;* in atmosphere and treatment, however, the play, though by far the more elaborately developed, resembles the other so closely that we may fairly consider them together, choosing our characteristic examples of Webster from either.

The first thing which reveals his inhibitory sense of fact is the amazing truth to actual life of his Italy. This is not a matter of historical detail. Webster makes as free with names and dates and recorded circumstances as any of his fellows made. But compare the Italy of Webster's *White Devil* with the France of Chapman's *Bussy*

Reprinted with the permission of Charles Scribner's Sons from The Temper of the Seventeenth Century, *pp. 85-88, by Barrett Wendell.*

d'Ambois—also less than thirty years past when the play about it was written. Chapman's France is an impalpable nowhere, peopled with stalking utterers of his full and heightened style; Webster's Italy, beside it, seems as accurately local as that of Stendhal. Again, compare this Italy of Webster's with that of Middleton, who—perhaps a little later—turned the story of Bianca Capello into *Women Beware Women*. For all Middleton's realism, his Florence is still a region not quite of fact, but of imagination too; a place to which one might have journeyed from Romeo's Verona or from Othello's Venice. By its side, Webster's Italy again reminds one of Stendhal's. Though it be fiction, it has a value almost documentary.

Now this Medicean Italy which he so faithfully tried to set forth was perhaps the most complex as well as the most corrupt region known to modern history. Intrigue within intrigue really marked it as the land which bred Machiavelli and thus gave our language an adjective to enshrine the memory of him. A sense of this complexity seems to have weighed down on Webster until it became benumbing; he always seems aware of how very much he has to tell, afraid lest he shall lose some thread of his labyrinthine argument, lest he shall unduly simplify deeds and characters which simplicity would belie. He never approaches unconscious ease; he never relaxes into sympathetic humor; there are no Nurses in his Italian world, or Mercutios. There are wonderful villains, though, and tenderly pathetic victims. The evil of life and the suffering—the horror and the sadness—he sets forth wonderfully. His work is full of isolated situations, and phrases, and touches of character and of aphorism, which seem almost ultimate in their combined power and truth to life. What makes the total effect of them bewildering is that he could never quite fuse them into organic unity. Again and again, he throws upon his readers the task of composing, if so they may, his marvellous fragments of tragedy. They are like some unfinished mosaic, needing a flash of electric fire to melt their outlines into the intelligible unity of painting.

E. E. Stoll

Malfi, last of [the] Kydian revenge-plays, is a long step ahead, both in the discarding of worn-out conventionalities, and in the harmonious development, after the stern Kydian spirit, of sombre, melodramatic setting, meditation, and style. It has no ghost, no poisoning-scene, no

From John Webster *by E. E. Stoll (Cambridge: Harvard Cooperative Society, 1905), pp. 118-19. Copyright 1905 by E. E. Stoll. Reprinted by permission of Mrs. Doris P. Franklin.*

conjuring, no revenger's soliloquy or feigned madness, no killing of the soul, or blood-curdling Latin. A revenger there is, a villain and a malcontent tool-villain, who is, as of old, ill-served; a multiplicity of omens and a prolonged torture-scene,—but all are newly treated. The convention of revenge as prime motive, long a-dying, is now dead; it no longer drew the sympathy of the audience to the hero; and, whereas in the *White Devil,* villains and hero had to be villains, in *Malfi* the place of the victim, hitherto held by the villain, is taken by the hero and the revenger, as the now prevailing moral and esthetic canons require, is represented as he *is*—a villain. The tool-villain, on the other hand, who, like Flamineo and unlike Malevole and Vendice, is tool-villain in his own character and not as a disguise, chooses, after being cheated, the better part, and avenges his victim. And the torture-scene—the torture of the heroine now, not of the villain—is made the center of interest and plot. Many old, specially Marstonian devices, also, are used anew. The tool-villain as torturer is disguised; omens, presentiments, and gloomy natural phenomena are introduced, not as with Tourneur for momentary, astounding effect, but, somewhat as with Marston, to infuse a vague, onward looking fear and dread; and meditations far more in the vein of Malevole than of Vendice, ethical and stoic ideas recalling Marston's, and satirical characterization are further developed. Spectacular and lyrical tendencies, moreover, in form somewhat like those of the *Second Maiden's Tragedy,* but of a sterner, more melancholy spirit, here come to their climax. There are the "noble ceremonies" of the cardinal's investiture as a warrior and of the banishment of the duchess, and the dumb-show of the wax figures of her dead husband and children; a dirge, two songs, a dance of madmen, and a weird Echo-scene. These, together with the brooding weight of omens and presentiments, a style encrusted with highly-wrought, sombre imagery, a setting of night and gloom, and a paraphernalia of torture and uncanny properties beyond example, give an effect of tragic environment and atmosphere more varied and complete than any hitherto on the melodramatic stage.

E. W. Hendy

. . . Webster seems to have found the dormouse an attractive little beast, as indeed he is. Perhaps he had kept one as a pet, for there are several allusions to his tractability and somnolence.

From *"John Webster: Playwright and Naturalist"* by *E. W. Hendy.* Nineteenth Century, *CIII (1928),* 117. *Copyright 1928 by* Nineteenth Century. *Reprinted by permission of* Twentieth Century.

Fredson Bowers

If Fletcher was the most influential playwright within this period, John Webster was the greatest and his treatment of the villain play the most thoroughly artistic. *The Duchess of Malfi* did not, as sometimes asserted, bring to a close the tradition of revenge tragedy. It did, however, provide in its plot structure the artistic climax to the particular type of drama which had been in the direct line of descent from Kyd and Marlowe, Marston and Tourneur, and marked the temporary discard of the much modified Kydian plot formula. Webster, together with Fletcher, is the bridge between the older Elizabethans and the so-called decadent drama of Massinger and Ford.

Webster's debt to Kydian tragedy in *The Duchess of Malfi* has been noted in detail—the wanton bloodshed, torture, use of the tool-villain, omens, and the like.[1] Only the structure of the plot and the position of the tool-villain will occupy us here. The play is peculiar in that the protagonist (the duchess herself) is the victim of the villains' revenge. This much and no more Webster found in his source. The problem, how to bring the guilty persons to justice, remained. If the death of the duchess were delayed until the dénouement, the villains in some inexplicable manner must become so involved as to bring disaster on their own heads or else be disposed of hugger-mugger by Antonio. The Kydian formula would suggest the murder of the duchess to be followed by the revenge of the distraught Antonio, but this would involve not only a decided wandering from the source but also a certain loss in the more pitiful and ironic aspects of the story. Webster clung to his source and accordingly was forced to create original machinery for his catastrophe, a task complicated by the loss of his major hero and the necessity for the early loss of his minor.

The solution came through the extension of the action of the tool-villain. Bosola is no mechanical villain of the Lorrique type. He is, instead, a misfit, a man of worthier talents forced into a degrading position and, with a brutal philosophy, making the most of it by the thoroughgoing manner in which he plays his part. If he must be a villain, one senses, he has decided to be an efficient one. Enough flashes of his independent better self are shown to stir the interest of the audience and the more to horrify them by the cynical brutality that

---

From Elizabethan Revenge Tragedy, 1587-1642 *by Fredson Bowers (Princeton: Princeton University Press, 1940), pp. 177-79. Copyright © 1940 by Princeton University Press. Reprinted by permission of the publisher.*

[1] E. E. Stoll, *John Webster*, pp. 93, 118-45.

follows. Indeed, Bosola has an almost surgical interest in torturing the human spirit to see how much it can endure before the veniality he seeks as the excuse for his existence is forced to the surface.

The unworldly bravery of the duchess proves to Bosola that his theories are false; but his character is so well conceived that his sympathies are not fully enrolled until he is made aware of the fate that awaits him at the hands of an ungrateful master. Already shaken by his experience with the duchess, he is cast completely adrift from his convictions by this second shock, and takes to himself the office of revenger for the duchess upon the men who have ruined him. With dramatic irony the first step in his new rôle is the unwitting murder of Antonio, the man whose life he had resolved to save. Bosola knows then that his life, tainted by years of evil, is doomed, and with that knowledge he becomes the impersonal agent of Death. In the mortal scuffle with his enemies that follows he meets his end, but not before he has seen one of his foes ironically slain and has with his own hand stabbed the second. The fatal retribution begun with the murder of the duchess has at last descended on the guilty parties.

This retribution is the keynote of the play, but it does not come from a Kydian revenger, for in a sense the villains bring it directly upon themselves. Ferdinand goes mad, the cardinal is no longer able to control his accomplice Bosola, and the resultant internecine strife works the havoc. The accomplice had always been the weak link in the Kydian villain's schemes. Webster followed the tradition of the weak link, but exalted the irony of the catastrophe and provided a more fitting doom for his villains by removing the element of accident from the accomplice's betrayal and founding such betrayal on a psychological change in character.

T. S. Eliot

I have not yet spoken of one very important reason why Webster's plays, in spite of their loose construction and incoherences, give a greater effect of unity than those of his contemporaries, and that is his greater gift of language. His plays are no more "literary" than those of the other late writers; indeed they are somewhat more carelessly written than some, but he had the gift of style. Even when he is imitating a situation already used by Shakespeare, his language is his own. There is, of course, a kind of common style to several of the Eliza-

From "The Duchess of Malfi" *by T. S. Eliot. Originally published in* The Listener, *XXVI (December 18, 1941), 825-26. Copyright © 1941 by T. S. Eliot. Reprinted by permission of Valerie Eliot.*

bethan dramatists, so that we cannot always be sure, even in fine passages, of the authorship: there were, for instance, commonplaces of words for the last speeches of heroes or villains when dying. But the playwright who had less of the native gift, only troubled to find the right word and phrase at the important moments: Webster has a natural overflowing gift for language, conspicuous in a time of rich and surprising phrase. John Addington Symonds, in his introduction to the Mermaid Edition of select plays of Webster and Tourneur, mentions some of the phrases characteristic of Webster; the poet of whom he most reminds us, in this gift of startling phrase, is John Donne. In comparing Webster to a poet who was not a dramatist, I do not mean to suggest that the value of his writing lies in the poetry and *not* in the drama. His verse is essentially dramatic verse, written for the theater by a man with a very acute sense of the theater. The later Elizabethan and the Jacobean poetry is forever brooding upon the more terrifying aspect of death, of the death of evil-doers, and of physical mortification and corruption. No doubt the recurrence of the plague in London, with all its incidental horrors, acted as a constant stimulant to this mortuary imagination: but in Donne, and to a less degree in the plays of Webster, there is a spiritual terror as well. The strange twinges of conscience of the Cardinal and Ferdinand, in *The Duchess of Malfy,* would almost make tragedy of these two characters by themselves, as of men divided between irresistible passions and unescapable nightmares, forced to act wickedly and yet in terror of damnation: almost, I say, because only the very greatest poet and dramatist could have risen to such a situation. Yet, though Webster is not among the very greatest, though he represents, as I have said, an artistic decline inevitable after the greatness of Shakespeare, I do not wish to leave you with the suspicion that his work shows also a *moral* decadence. In a world without meaning there can still be horror, but not tragedy. Webster's drama is tragic, and belongs to a world in which right and wrong, the soul and its destiny, are still the most important things.

F. P. Wilson

Both Chapman and Jonson write for the public theaters, but they make few concessions to popular taste. Jonson's aim was to keep tragedy "high and aloof," and Chapman while basing his plots mainly

From Elizabethan and Jacobean *by F. P. Wilson (London: The Clarendon Press, 1945), pp. 104-106. Copyright © 1945 by the Clarendon Press. Reprinted by permission of the publisher.*

on contemporary French history infused into them the spirit of Stoic morality, and preserved in his use of the messenger and the long set speech some of the technical characteristics of Senecan drama. There is, however, another line of drama, less learned and more popular, though retaining many Senecan traits, which descends from Kyd's *Spanish Tragedy* through *Hamlet* and the revenge plays of Marston to Tourneur and Webster. It is here that some critics have found the finest examples of dramatic poetry outside Shakespeare, while others, repelled by the preoccupation of these dramatists with lust and crime and death, have likened the reading of their plays to a visit to the chamber of horrors in Madame Tussaud's. I will not say with Mr. F. L. Lucas that the only answer to those who say "But people do not do such things" as are done in the plays of Tourneur and Webster is: "They did. . . . Read the history of the time," especially the history of Renaissance Italy; I will not argue on these lines, for to do so might suggest that the action in these plays was naturalistic. Perhaps the modern reader has to make certain adjustments: to remember, for example, that that age believed in omens and portents, not tepidly and sporadically, but profoundly, so that the effect of the prodigious storm when Essex left London for Ireland "with furious flashings, the firmament seeming to open and burn" was such that Florio recorded it in his Italian-English dictionary; to remember that the Jacobeans, as the Elizabethans, inherited from the later Middle Ages a preoccupation with death which seems to us abnormal. Their lives were guarded about with symbols of dissolution; the death's head and the *memento mori* were still in vogue. An illustration may make this clear. When the Duchess of Malfi is to be strangled at the order of her brothers, and the executioners enter with a coffin, cords, and a bell, the bellman is impersonated by Bosola, the half-willing, half-reluctant tool of the brothers:

> I am the common Bellman
> That usually is sent to condemn'd persons
> The night before they suffer.

The reference is to a charity presented in 1605 by a rich citizen of London to the church of St. Sepulchre's hard by the prison of Newgate. Money was given for the making of a speech outside the dungeon of condemned prisoners the night before their execution, and for another speech to be made the next morning, while the cart in which the prisoners made their melancholy progress to Tyburn was stayed for a while by the church wall. The words of both speeches are set out in the gift, as also is the refrain, accompanied by a tolling handbell, *Our Lord Take Mercy Upon You All.* Documents like these illustrate the gulf in taste between that age and this. It has not been

noticed that one of the signatories to this gift is a John Webster,
but the name is too common for us to be sure that he is the dramatist.
Those who confuse Webster's plays with *The Police News* will say
that there could be no more appropriate document for him to sign
and no more appropriate church for him to worship in than St.
Sepulchre's. Yet let us notice that in his play Webster says nothing to
recall the speeches of the charity but gives to bellman Bosola verses
which express in universal terms the desire for death after overwhelm-
ing suffering.

> Hark now every thing is still.
> The Scritch-Owl, and the whistler shrill
> Call upon our Dame, aloud,
> And bid her quickly don her shroud.
> Much you had of land and rent,
> Your length in clay's now competent.
> A long war disturb'd your mind,
> Here your perfect peace is sign'd.
> Of what is't fools make such vain keeping?
> Sin their conception, their birth, weeping,
> Their life, a general mist of error,
> Their death, a hideous storm of terror.
> Strew your hair with powders sweet:
> Don clean linen, bathe your feet,
> And (the foul fiend more to check)
> A crucifix let bless your neck.
> 'Tis now full tide, 'tween night and day,
> End your groan, and come away.

There is no gulf in feeling between us and this kind of writing, and
the gruesome apparatus which Tourneur and Webster find necessary
should not come between us and the power of their poetry.

Willard Farnham

As the Renaissance proceeded with its discovery of intrinsic worth
in mundane life, it fostered in many men the thought that the world
should be more perfect and the hope that it could be more perfect.
In having this thought and this hope, men laid themselves open to
the danger of disillusionment, and when disillusionment came, it frequently found expression—especially in the late Renaissance—in terms

From Shakespeare's Tragic Frontier *by Willard Farnham (Berkeley: University of
California Press, 1950), pp. 131-32. Copyright © 1950 by the Regents of the University of California. Reprinted by permission of the publisher.*

of medieval contempt of the world altered to suit a new spirit. At
such times the grave and all things leading to the grave wore an aspect
they had not possessed when faith had fixed men's hope and desire
upon the next world. "Do we affect fashion in the grave?" asks the
Duchess in Webster's *Duchess of Malfi*. "Most ambitiously," answers
Bosola; for, as he goes on to say with wistful bitterness, the medieval
fashion of showing hopeful desire for heaven is now no longer followed, and in accordance with a new fashion of funerary sculpture,

> Princes images on their tombes
> Do not lie, as they were wont, seeming to pray
> Up to heaven: but with their hands under their cheekes,
> (As if they died of the tooth-ache)—they are not carved
> With their eies fix'd upon the starres; but as
> Their mindes were wholy bent upon the world,
> The selfe-same way they seeme to turne their faces.

The dark tragedies of Shakespeare may not show him as a man disillusioned by his experiences, but they certainly show him as one
deeply concerned with questions that would never have been raised if
the Renaissance had never been disillusioned by the world, in other
words, if the Renaissance had not upon occasion lost its guiding faith
in the world and turned to despair of the world.

Herbert J. Muller

Webster's tense, ambiguous vision of life is summed up in his treatment of death. No Elizabethan playwright seems more obsessed with
the theme, or insists so morbidly on the earthworms whom man lives
to feed. None strews the stage with more corpses at less provocation.
The often weak motivation for the killings emphasizes the irrational
evil that makes his world so nightmarish. Yet it is in death that
Webster's characters realize themselves, summon up the best of their
humanity. Even his villains usually meet it with dignity. As one says,

> I do glory yet
> That I can call this act mine own.

A nobler character states the essential faith of tragedy:

> Though in our miseries Fortune have a part,
> Yet in our noble sufferings she hath none:
> Contempt of pain, that we may call our own.

From The Spirit of Tragedy *by Herbert J. Muller (New York: Alfred A. Knopf,
Inc., 1956), pp. 198-99. Copyright © 1956 by Alfred A. Knopf, Inc. Reprinted by
permission of the publisher.*

Altogether, Webster's tragedies are second only to Shakespeare's. *The Duchess of Malfi,* produced shortly after Shakespeare had quit the stage, made a grand enough swan song for Elizabethan tragedy. It is the more mournful, however, because the death of this tragedy seems premature. The qualities of greatness in Webster throw into sharper relief the serious faults that he never outgrew. His crudities make him seem irresponsible in spite of his basic sincerity, even his desperate earnestness. And his qualities of desperation point to his limited command—intellectual or imaginative—of a tragic condition that made him feel so intensely. He was shocked, obsessed, by an evil that he could not transcend in a larger frame or a longer perspective.

Although this sense of evil may be traced to the medieval heritage, the pessimism of Webster does not seem medieval. The many references to heaven and hell sound as conventional as the many to Fortune; they are not tense with religious feeling. The hell that concerned him was here on earth, and heaven was evidently no compensation for it. Ultimately, his pessimism—and that of Tourneur—seems due to disillusionment with Renaissance ideals. It signified a loss of faith rather than a reassertion of the traditional faith, and so took the form of a violent revulsion. Its most apparent source, or symbol, was the growing rule of money, in a society that was shifting from a feudal to a capitalistic economy. Like other Elizabethans, Webster and Tourneur attacked the Machiavellian politician, but they harped most of all on the theme of greed, the evils of gold. As most Americans know, "Business and sentiment don't mix." Many Elizabethans were still naïve enough to believe that sentiment was more important.

L. G. Salingar

Unlike Vittoria, the Duchess of Malfi is almost blameless. A young widow, she remarries beneath her, secretly, and against her brothers' wishes; but these blemishes on her conduct, stressed in Webster's narrative source, are almost unfelt in his portrayal of her gracious charm, shining out beside her brothers' blackness. Yet she, too, is pursued by guilt, by a premonition of disaster, even in her wooing:

> You do tremble:
> Make not your heart so dead a piece of flesh,
> To fear more than to love me. Sir, be confident:

From "Tourneur and the Tragedy of Revenge" by L. G. Salingar. From The Age of Shakespeare, ed. Boris Ford, Vol. II of The Pelican Guide to English Literature (Baltimore: Penguin Books Inc., 1956; London: Penguin Books Ltd., 1956), pp. 351-53. Copyright © 1956 by Penguin Books Ltd. Reprinted by permission of the publisher.

> What is't distracts you? This is flesh and blood, sir;
> 'Tis not the figure cut in alabaster
> Kneels at my husband's tomb.
>
> (I.1)

This lends a kind of allegorical fitness to her long-drawn-out torments (Act IV), which bring her "by degrees to mortification," but
which otherwise deserve Shaw's gibe at Webster as "Tussaud lau-
reate." Webster's finest sustained writing conveys with terrible imme-
diacy her exhaustion and yearning to escape from consciousness:

> I'll tell thee a miracle—
> I am not mad yet, to my cause of sorrow.
> Th' heaven o'er my heart seems made of molten brass,
> The earth of flaming sulphur, yet I am not mad:
> I am acquainted with sad misery
> As the tann'd galley-slave is with his Oar;
> Necessity makes me suffer constantly,
> And custom makes it easy.—Who do I look like now?   (IV. ii)

Like the quarrel scene, however, this poignant declamation has no
further effect on the moral scheme of the play. It marks the limit of
Webster's insight; and the closing question (which invites the maid's
comparison with "reverend monuments") indicates his habitual fall-
ing back on showmanship. The remainder of the action consists of
tedious moralizing, posturing, and blood-and-thunder.

But Webster's determination to maneuver his characters into a trap
is most evident with the two scholar-villains, Flamineo and Bosola,
who combine this role with that of malcontent satirist. Evidently
Webster felt uneasy with this unlifelike stage convention,[1] which
belongs to the impersonal mode of "humour" comedy; his satirists
are more introspective and more mannered than their predecessors
in Marston and Tourneur, but also more disjointed—Flamineo's
temptation scene, for instance, is a hollow echo of Vindice's, and
Bosola's disquisition on women's painting is gratuitous and nasty.
Their strongest satiric note is the horror of economic "necessity":
Flamineo, with his bragging defiance on behalf of

> the beggary of courtiers,
> The discontent of churchmen, want of soldiers,
> And all the creatures that hang manacled,
> Worse than strappadoed, on the lowest felly
> Of Fortune's wheel,

---

[1] See Flamineo's speech: "It may appear to some ridiculous / Thus to talk knave
and madman. . . ." (*White Devil*, IV. ii).

which is varied, through "all the weary minutes" of his life, with his anxiety about renewed poverty and neglect; or Bosola demanding "Who would rely on these miserable dependancies, in expectation to be advanced tomorrow? what creature ever fed worse than hoping Tantalus?" Yet each is made to forfeit his hard-gained experience, as well as his conscience, in order to return to that very situation; their parts are manipulated so as to ring the changes on cynicism and remorse. And their sense of futility is extended to other characters as well. Later, in *The Devil's Law Case* (1619-20) and *Appius and Virginia* (c. 1630), Webster returns again to themes of "impossible desire" and situations where "pity would destroy pity." Haunted by his predecessors' conception of moral law, he can neither accept nor amend it; in a world he sees as corrupt through and through, he can only exploit his own discomfort.

Behind *The Revenger's Tragedy* are traditional ideas and attitudes of mind which were shared by the public as a whole in their life outside the theater; with all its violent personal feeling, the drama does no more than give these public traditions flesh and blood. Webster's agitation and Webster's subtlety show the emergence of a new kind of tragedy, more romantic and more narrowly theatrical. But the kernel of Elizabethan popular tradition has crumbled away, and only the husk remains.

Frank W. Wadsworth

To recapitulate the arguments which have been advanced. First, it seems at variance with the evidence to assume, as Dr. Leech does that Webster's audience would have unhesitatingly and without qualification condemned the Duchess of Malfi for remarrying or for marrying beneath herself. Second, it seems even more unwarrantable to assume on the basis of incomplete evidence lying outside the play that Webster condemns the Duchess. In fact, when we examine her case on its own merits, there are indications that Webster's attitude towards his protagonist was diametrically opposed to what Dr. Leech assumes it to have been. These are, first, the efforts on Webster's part to convince his audience that the Duchess' motives for remarrying are praiseworthy and respectable (i.e., love rather than lust); and second, his attempts to show that the object of her choice was, in spite of his birth, an ideally acceptable husband.

From "*Webster's* Duchess of Malfi *in the Light of Some Contemporary Ideas on Marriage and Remarriage*," *by Frank W. Wadsworth.* Philological Quarterly, *XXXV (1956), 407. Copyright © 1956 by University of Iowa Press. Reprinted by permission of the* Philological Quarterly.

The necessity of understanding the Duchess' motives correctly is obvious. Unlike *The White Devil,* where the tragic focus is on more than one figure, *The Duchess of Malfi* is essentially the heroine's play, and this in spite of the fact that she is killed at the end of Act IV. To fail to understand either her, or Webster's attitude towards her, causes Webster's already careless workmanship to seem, as Dr. Leech's study demonstrates, chaotically inept. Even worse, to visualize the tragedy as "a warning to the rash and the wanton," as Dr. Leech suggests that we should, is to destroy its essential significance, for if *The Duchess of Malfi* is seen simply as a "warning," Webster's powerful and disturbing pessimism dwindles to conventional didacticism, and the dramatist who in Eliot's words reveals the skull beneath the skin fades to a mere purveyor of candy goodness.

Northrop Frye

The phases of tragedy move from the heroic to the ironic, the first three corresponding to the first three phases of romance, the last three to the last three of irony. The first phase of tragedy is the one in which the central character is given the greatest possible dignity in contrast to the other characters, so that we get the perspective of a stag pulled down by wolves. The sources of dignity are courage and innocence, and in this phase the hero or heroine usually is innocent. This phase corresponds to the myth of the birth of the hero in romance, a theme which is occasionally incorporated into a tragic structure, as in Racine's *Athalie.* But owing to the unusual difficulty of making an interesting dramatic character out of an infant, the central and typical figure of this phase is the calumniated woman, often a mother the legitimacy of whose child is suspected. A whole series of tragedies based on a Griselda figure belong here, stretching from the Senecan *Octavia* to Hardy's Tess, and including the tragedy of Hermione in *The Winter's Tale.* If we are to read *Alcestis* as a tragedy, we have to see it as a tragedy of this phase in which Alcestis is violated by Death and then has her fidelity vindicated by being restored to life. *Cymbeline* belongs here too: in this play the theme of the birth of the hero appears offstage, for Cymbeline was the king of Britain at the time of the birth of Christ, and the halcyon peace in which the play concludes has a suppressed reference to this. An even clearer example, and certainly one of the greatest in English literature, is *The Duchess of Malfi.* The Duchess has the inno-

From The Anatomy of Criticism *by Northrop Frye (Princeton: Princeton University Press, 1957), pp. 219-20. Copyright © 1957 by Princeton University Press. Reprinted by permission of the publishers.*

cence of abundant life in a sick and melancholy society, where the
fact that she has "youth and a little beauty" is precisely why she is
hated. She reminds us too that one of the essential characteristics of
innocence in the martyr is an unwillingness to die. When Bosola
comes to murder her he makes elaborate attempts to put her half in
love with easeful death and to suggest that death is really a deliver-
ance. The attempt is motivated by a grimly controlled pity, and is
roughly the equivalent of the vinegar sponge in the Passion. When
the Duchess, her back to the wall, says "I am the Duchess of Malfi
still," "still" having its full weight of "always," we understand how
it is that even after her death her invisible presence continues to be
the most vital character in the play. *The White Devil* is an ironic
parody-treatment of the same phase.

C. G. Thayer

To recapitulate: the first and most consistent salient fact about
Bosola is his ambiguity. This is established at the beginning of the
play, and throughout the early scenes it expands, takes on new di-
mensions. In III. v, the Duchess refers to his counterfeit face; in IV. ii,
he appears in disguise, is compared to a good actor playing a villain's
part, removes his disguise, and henceforth devotes his life to atone-
ment. After the murder of the Duchess, Bosola emerges as a changed
man, or, more accurately, emphasis is placed on aspects of his character which had only been suggested earlier. Webster has objectified
this new emphasis in two statements of Bosola's about the stars:
"Look you, the stars shine still," he sardonically tells the Duchess
when she would curse them. When he accidentally kills Antonio he
speaks of the stars again, but from a very different point of view:
"We are meerely the Starres tennys-balls (strooke, and banded / Which
way please them)—" (v. iv. 63-64). In Webster's universe, this constitutes a part of wisdom, and it is ironic that with this knowledge
Bosola must still pursue his fatal path of right. This path will of
course lead him to get revenge on Ferdinand and the Cardinal and
in doing so to meet his own death. Toward the close of the play, he
explains his motives:

> Revenge, for the Duchesse of Malfy, murdered
> By th'Aragonian brethren: for Antonio,
> Slaine by [t]his hand: for lustfull Julia,

From "The Ambiguity of Bosola" by C. G. Thayer. Studies in Philology, LIV
(1957), 170-71. Copyright © 1957 by the University of North Carolina Press. Reprinted by permission of Studies in Philology.

> Poyson'd by this man: and lastly, for my selfe,
> (That was an Actor in the maine of all,
> Much 'gainst mine owne good nature, yet i'th'end
> Neglected.) (v. v. 102-108)

The total impression seems to be of Bosola slowly, definitely emerging from a kind of moral and intellectual disguise early in the play, to a genuine understanding of his true identity at the end of iv. ii, to a final personal redemption at the end of the play. His disguise in the murder scene seems to objectify the problem of his identity. It seems to mean not only that in the murder scene he is symbolically *not* the Bosola we see later, but to suggest that the true Bosola has only been glimpsed before, never clearly seen. In the most dramatic and moving scene of the play (iv. ii), he removes his disguise and emerges with his evil qualities gone and only his good qualities— "mine own good nature"—remaining. The idea of Bosola as an actor, with a counterfeit face and a disguise, with his and Ferdinand's references to himself as an actor, is entirely consistent with the ambiguous preliminary presentation of the character in the words of Antonio and Delio at the beginning of the play.

With respect to his own tragedy, Bosola's emergence may be described as follows: as a kind of cynical act of rebellion against an evil universe, he pursues an evil course himself, rationalizing it in terms of gratitude and devotion to Ferdinand. He learns, through observing the suffering of the Duchess and through his other experiences, the virtue of her passiveness and a somewhat more masculine, active concept, which is that even in an evil universe one must remain virtuous—true to himself—and actively labor for what appears right. One must not only *see* himself: one must *be* himself. This, in Malraux's famous phrase, is *la condition humaine*; and this is one of the facts which give tragic significance to human life. So Bosola seems to suggest, in his dying words:

> . . . Oh this gloomy world,
> In what a shadow, or deepe pit of darkness,
> Doth (womanish, and feareful) mankind live!
> Let worthy mindes nere stagger in distrust
> To suffer death or shame, for what is just— (v. v. 124-128)

Bosola emerges then as a kind of baroque figure, struggling against an unyielding, darkly beautiful universe which produces evil, insists on virtue, but ultimately destroys evil and virtue alike. For Webster and for others, this is certainly man's tragic fate.

Seymour L. Gross

That Webster is the most powerful dramatic poet after Shakespeare is, I imagine, beyond dispute; but the moral point of view which informs his great works has been, it seems to me, much misconstrued. Rupert Brooke's description of Webster's characters as "writhing grubs in an immense night" has, so it seems, so conditioned subsequent critical judgment that even Webster's most recent commentator, Dr. Travis Bogard, asserts that "in Webster's world . . . Evil and good are dragged down together in death, just as they are meshed together in life. The only triumph comes when, even in the moment of defeat, an individual is roused to assert his own integrity of life. *This is not a question of virtue and vice.* In Webster's tragic world, characters are significant not because of their morality but because of their struggle." [1]

Non-moral tragedy, as posited here for Webster, is an untenable proposition. As Professor Henry Meyers reminds us, tragedy is neither pessimistic nor optimistic, but is, rather, "a spectacle of a constant and inevitable relation between good and evil, a dramatic presentation of a law of values." [2] That the Websterian character's struggle for "integrity of life," despite the horror and cynicism which suffuses the plays, is not divorced from the traditional polarities of good and evil can be made quite clear by looking, even briefly, at the greatest of Webster's plays—*The Duchess of Malfi.*

Dr. Bogard quotes the final couplet of *The Duchess of Malfi* as the "summing-up" of Webster's idea that "integrity of life cuts across the traditional evaluative divisions of good and evil, and proves, in the final synthesis, to be the sole standard of positive ethical judgment in the tragedies." (p. 40.) The couplet should not, however, be quoted out of context, for the two preceding lines sharply qualify it.

> Nature doth nothing so great for great men
> As when she's pleas'd to make them lords of truth:
> Integrity of life is fame's best friend,
> Which nobly, beyond death, shall crown the end.

Clearly, this means that integrity of life is essentially bound up with some kind of positive moral value, here signified as "truth"; the whole of *The Duchess of Malfi* bears this out.

From *"A Note on Webster's Tragic Attitude"* by *Seymour L. Gross.* Notes and Queries, *Vol. 202 (1957), 374-75. Copyright © 1957 by Oxford University Press. Reprinted by permission of Oxford University Press.*

[1] *The Tragic Satire of John Webster* (Berkeley, 1955), p. 79. (My italics.)
[2] *Tragedy: A View of Life* (Ithaca, 1956), p. 8.

Why is it that the Duchess never loses our sympathy? Is it not because she never violates what might be generally signified as moral goodness? Certainly her triumph over oppression and fear is a tragic victory not because she has maintained her integrity of life, but rather because her integrity involves courage ("Pull, and pull strongly, for your able strength / Must pull down heaven upon me"); humility ("heaven-gates are not so highly arch'd / As princes' palaces; they that enter there / Must go upon their knees"); and a huge capacity for selflessness, which even at the point of death prompts her to say, "I pray thee, look thou givest my little boy / Some syrup for his cold." The point is even clearer in the two brothers. Surely Ferdinand, until Act IV, is more gruesome than his brother the Cardinal. His pathologically brutal treatment of his sister, culminating in the ex-quisite tortures he devises for killing her body and shattering her soul, certainly horrifies us more than the Cardinal's frigid Machia-vellism. Yet it is Ferdinand, not his brother, who finally elicits our sympathies, for of the two only he finally struggles towards some morally oriented integrity of life. His famous utterance—"Cover her face; mine eyes dazzle; she died young"—is the inception of a struggle towards goodness—a struggle, it turns out, which ends in madness. But even his madness is a kind of triumph, for we can recognize its source as being moral self-revulsion. The Cardinal also struggles to maintain his integrity of life, but because for him this only involves a fight to hold on to the fruits of his viciousness, because he never retreats from evil, when he dies he is merely defeated. The Cardinal dies wishing only to be forgotten; Ferdinand with the words "O my sister" on his lips. Surely the difference in effect is very much "a ques-tion of virtue and vice."

But perhaps the clearest refutation of a non-moral tragic vision in Webster is to be found in Bosola's final speech (usually quoted only in part as an example of Webster's moral despair):

> O, this gloomy world!
> In what a shadow, or deep pit of darkness,
> Doth womanish and fearful mankind live!
> Let worthy minds ne're stagger in distrust
> To suffer death or shame for what is just:
> Mine is another voyage.

Who should know better than Bosola, an essentially moral man who has yielded to the pressures of corruption, that the only thing which makes the struggle for integrity of life meaningful is its direction. His final knowledge that he has not suffered death and shame for what is just, that he has suffered them for nothing, is an agonized testa-ment of faith in the moral structure of the world. In his "Mine is

another voyage," there is both a history of grief and the moral center
of Websterian tragedy.

F. L. Lucas

Its plot as a whole has added nothing to the greatness of *The
Duchess of Malfi*: but neither can it destroy it. We turn back from
the critics, from Lamb with his outcries of admiration, from Archer
with his nibbling pedantries, from Stoll and Kiesow with their vision
of the play as a warning of the awful results of marrying beneath
one, to the poet himself.

> 'Tis weakenesse,
> Too much to thinke what should have bin done.

Let us be thankful for what has been—for this picture of a spirit that
faces the cold shining of the stars with none of Pascal's terror before
their infinite silence, and the mopping and mowing of the demented
world around it with a calm that prosperity could not give, nor disaster
take away.

From The Duchess of Malfi, *ed. F. L. Lucas, (London: Chatto and Windus Ltd.,
1958), pp. 34-35. Copyright © 1958 by F. L. Lucas. Reprinted by permission of the
publisher and the Estate of F. L. Lucas.*

Chronology of Important Dates

c. 1580? John Webster born; the date is conjectural and the place unknown.

1602 May: Henslowe's diary notes payments to Webster, among a group of playwrights, for his contribution to various plays.

1603 Queen Elizabeth I died and was succeeded by King James I. The first quarto of *Hamlet* was published. Plague in London.

1604 Induction to Marston's *Malcontent*; the play was first acted by the Blackfriars boys, and Webster's addition marks the first performance by the King's Men.

1605 *Northward Ho!*, with Dekker. Gunpowder Plot.

1608 The King's Men merged with the Blackfriars boys; Shakespeare wrote his last tragedies, *Antony and Cleopatra* and *Coriolanus*. John Milton born.

1610? *The Devil's Law Case*, a tragicomedy by Webster published in 1623; the date is conjectural, and the play may be later than 1610.

1611 Shakespeare retired to Stratford. Donne, *Anatomy of the World*.

1612 *The White Devil* published (written 1609-1612?). Webster contributed verses to "his beloued friend Maister Thomas Heywood" to the latter's *Apology for Actors*.

1613-4 *The Duchess of Malfi* (revised 1617-23? published 1623).

1615 Contributed thirty-two new characters to the sixth edition of Overbury's *Characters*.

1616 Shakespeare and Francis Beaumont died. Jonson published his *Works*. William Harvey expounded the circulation of the blood.

1623 Shakespeare, First Folio.

1624 *Monuments of Honour*, a pageant for the inauguration of merchant-tailor John Gore, published by "Iohn Webster Merchant-Taylor." *The Late Murder of the Sun Upon the Mother, or Keep the Widow Waking*, a lost play on which Webster collaborated with Dekker, Ford, and Rowley.

c. 1624-5   *A Cure for a Cuckold,* with Rowley and perhaps Heywood.

1625   Accession of King Charles I. Plague in London.

c. 1627   *Appius and Virginia,* perhaps with Heywood.

1634   November: died—or he may have done so in March 1638, or at an unknown third time.

Notes on the Editor and Contributors

NORMAN RABKIN, the editor of this volume, is Associate Professor of English and Associate Dean of the College of Letters and Science at the University of California, Berkeley. He received his Ph.D. from Harvard; he is the author of *Shakespeare and the Common Understanding* (1967), editor of *Approaches to Shakespeare* (1964), and co-editor with Max Bluestone of *Shakespeare's Contemporaries: Modern Studies in English Renaissance Drama*.

WILLIAM ARCHER (1856-1924) shared with George Bernard Shaw the apostleship of Ibsen in England. Author of numerous works on the theater, he was a playwright himself, and translated Ibsen.

TRAVIS BOGARD is Professor of Dramatic Art at the University of California, Berkeley and co-editor, with William I. Oliver, of *Modern Drama: Essays in Criticism*.

FREDSON T. BOWERS, Chairman of the Department of English at the University of Virginia, has written a number of books on bibliographical and textual problems in sixteenth and seventeenth century literature, especially drama, and in nineteenth century American literature; and he has edited a good deal of Renaissance drama.

MURIEL C. BRADBROOK, Reader in English at Cambridge University, has written many books on Renaissance and modern theater and numerous other literary matters, both English and continental.

RUPERT BROOKE (1887-1915), one of the most notable casualties of the first World War, was by the time of his death already an accomplished poet. His book on Webster, written when he was twenty-four, won him a fellowship at King's College, Cambridge.

JAMES L. CALDERWOOD teaches at the University of California, Irvine, and has written extensively on Shakespeare.

T. S. ELIOT (1888-1965) was as influential in his criticism as in his poetry, and played a considerable part in the revival of interest in Renaissance drama.

UNA ELLIS-FERMOR (1894-1958), Professor of English at the University of London, was General Editor of the New Arden Shakespeare from 1951 until her death; she wrote many books, notably *Christopher Marlowe, The Frontiers of Drama,* and *Shakespeare the Dramatist.*

WILLIAM EMPSON, Professor of English Literature at Sheffield University, has had enormous influence on criticism. His books include *Seven Types of Ambiguity, Some Versions of Pastoral, The Structure of Complex Words,* and *Milton's God.*

WILLARD FARNHAM, Professor Emeritus of English at the University of California, Berkeley, is author of *The Medieval Heritage of Elizabethan Tragedy* and editor of the Pelican *Hamlet.*

NORTHROP FRYE is Professor of English at Victoria College, University of Toronto, author of a number of books, and an influential literary theorist.

CLIFFORD LEECH, Chairman of the Department of English at University College, Toronto, has published many books on Shakespeare and the drama, particularly that of the seventeeth century and including *John Webster* (1961). He is general editor of the Revels Plays.

F. L. LUCAS (1894-1967) was a Fellow of King's College, Cambridge. Translator, poet, playwright, essayist, he wrote a number of books covering an extraordinary range of world literature and literary problems. He edited *The Complete Works of John Webster* (1927).

HERBERT J. MULLER, author of *The Uses of the Past* and other books on such matters as science, freedom in the ancient world, religion and freedom in the modern world, and Adlai Stevenson, is Distinguished Service Professor at Indiana University.

ROBERT ORNSTEIN is Chairman of the Department of English at Western Reserve University. He has edited *Discussions of Shakespeare's Problem Comedies* and, with Hazelton Spencer, *Elizabethan and Jacobean Tragedy and Comedy.*

E. E. STOLL (1874-1959) was a pioneer rebel against nineteenth century Shakespeare criticism and a pioneer historian of Elizabethan drama.

C. G. THAYER, Professor of English at Ohio University, has written *Ben Jonson: Studies in the Plays.*

FRANK W. WADSWORTH is Dean of the Division of Humanities at the University of Pittsburgh and author of *The Poacher from Stratford* and other studies of Renaissance literature.

BARRETT WENDELL (1855-1921), Professor at Harvard, was a novelist, social critic, and historian of American, English, and European literature.

F. P. WILSON (1889-1963) was Merton Professor of English Literature in Oxford. General Editor of the Malone Society, co-editor of The Oxford History of English Literature, he was author of *Marlowe and the Early Shakespeare* and other studies in Renaissance literature.

Selected Bibliography

Allison, Alexander W., "Ethical Themes in *The Duchess of Malfi*," *Studies in English Literature 1500-1900*, IV (1964), 263-74. A thematic interpretation which presents the tragedy as affirmative not because the Duchess sins against degree (though her "eroticism" is her "flaw"), but because evil is self-defeating.

Boklund, Gunnar, *The Duchess of Malfi: Sources, Themes, Characters*. Cambridge, Mass.: Harvard University Press, 1962. Particularly valuable for its evaluation of the play's indebtedness to its sources.

Boyer, C. V., *The Villain as Hero in Elizabethan Tragedy*. London: George Routledge & Sons, Ltd.; New York: E. P. Dutton & Co. Inc., 1914. Pages 151-64. A study of Bosola as a combination of the malcontent, tool-villain, and revenger, who fails as dramatic character because "his struggle with moral law is not of sufficient magnitude."

Brennan, Elizabeth, "The Relationship Between Brother and Sister in the Plays of John Webster," *Modern Language Review*, LVIII (1963), 488-94. Argues that an incestuously jealous Ferdinand plays the role of revenging husband to cloak his passion, and that Webster thus characteristically plays on and surprises the audience's conventional expectations.

Brown, John Russell, ed., *The Duchess of Malfi*. The Revels Plays, London: Methuen & Co. Ltd.; Cambridge, Mass.: Harvard University Press, 1964. The best edition of the play, fully annotated, with numerous scholarly aids and an excellent introduction.

Dent, R. W., *John Webster's Borrowing*. Berkeley and Los Angeles: University of California Press, 1960. An exhaustive investigation of Webster's use of borrowed literary materials.

Jack, Ian, "The Case of John Webster," *Scrutiny*, XVI (1959), 38-53. An impassioned attack on Webster's decadence, moral and aesthetic.

Luecke, Jane Marie, O.S.B., "*The Duchess of Malfi*: Comic and Satiric Confusion in a Tragedy," *Studies in English Literature 1500-1900*, IV (1964), 275-90. A discussion of the problematic mingling of tragedy, satire, and comedy in the play.

Moore, Don D., *John Webster and His Critics, 1617-1964*. Baton Rouge: Louisiana State University Press, 1966. A history of Webster's reputation with a useful bibliography.

Mulryne, J. R., " 'The White Devil' and 'The Duchess of Malfi,' " in *Jacobean Drama*, Stratford-Upon-Avon Studies, I (1960), pp. 214-25. A sensitive study, particularly valuable in its account of the coherence and of the style of the play.

Praz, Mario, "John Webster and *The Maid's Tragedy*," *English Studies*, XXXVII (1956), 252-58. A suggestive demonstration of the indebtedness of *The Duchess of Malfi* to Beaumont and Fletcher's brilliant but meretricious tragedy.

Price, Hereward T., "The Function of Imagery in Webster," *Publications of the Modern Language Association*, LXX (1955), 717-39. A study of the relation between imagery and action.

Prior, Moody E., *The Language of Tragedy*. New York: Columbia University Press, 1947. Pages 120-35. A demonstration of the ordered design underlying the imagery of the play.

Riewald, J. G., "Shakespeare Burlesque in John Webster's *The Duchess of Malfi*," in *English Studies Presented to R. W. Zandvoort*, Amsterdam, 1964, pages 177-89. An investigation of the indebtedness of the doctor's scene to Lady Macbeth's sleepwalking, arguing that Webster's borrowings from contemporary drama are "macro-structural" as well as verbal.